CHRIST-CONFIDENT

Finally Placing Our
Confidence in the Right ONE

CURTIS BRACY

Published in the United States by Curtis Bracy

Consulted by Lighthouse Consulting, a Division of Carr Corp Enterprises

Paperback ISBN: 978-0-578-39811-2
Ebook ISBN: 978-1-0880-1851-4

Cover design & interior design by: Charlyn D.
Cover photograph by Malcolm Smiley
(Malcolm Smiley Studios)

All scripture quotations are from the KJV, NLT, ESV, NASB, AMP, MSG, CSB, and NKJV.

CONTENTS

FOREWORD

he first time I met the author, Elder Curtis Bracy, I immediately noticed his size, demeanor, and the way he carries himself. Elder Bracy is serious about his relationship with the Lord. He has proven that he is a dedicated student of the word of God. When he first came to the Lighthouse Temple Church, he was adamant about being baptized in the name of Lord Jesus Christ. Affectionately known in the body of Christ as "The Warfare Preacher" from that time to now, he has been clear about God's purpose and mission in his life.

It is no surprise that Curtis Bracy's second book would be called *Christ-Confident: Finally Placing Our Confidence in the Right One*. The scripture tells us in Joshua 1:9, "Have I not commanded you? Be strong and courageous. Do not be afraid; do not be discouraged, for the Lord your God will be with you wherever you go." This book encourages us to do just that. One part of the book that stood out to me was when Elder Bracy said he strongly believes "that God does not bring us into a new territory to blend in; He brings us on to change the atmosphere." Much like the author, this book is a game-changer.

As the Senior Pastor of the Lighthouse Temple Church, I have seen firsthand what has occurred in the last two and a half years because of the pandemic. Families throughout this great country and the world have experienced a tsunami of issues that affect our mental health. While these issues have been around for years, the pandemic has forced us to question, how are we going to deal with them? The author points out in this book that suicide, self-harm, PSTD, drug and alcohol addiction, child abandonment, and many other disorders seem insurmountable. However, Elder Bracy offers us a panacea and examples based on the scriptures for our benefit.

Elder Bracy shows us that there is a difference between self-confidence and Christ-confidence. Jesus said in John 10:10, "The thief does not come except to steal, and to kill, and to destroy. I have come that they may have life and that they may have it more abundantly".

With the turn of every page, I found myself engaged and eager to finish. I pray that reading this book allows you the same opportunity.

As a pastor, I will surely keep this book on my shelf as a bridge from clinical science to biblical applications. Elder Bracy provides examples in each chapter that make this text applicable to all ages. It is my sincere prayer that the same Holy Spirit that inspired Elder Bracy to write this book, ministers to you as you read and study this text. May we all be Christ Confident!

Pastor Mark E. Parrott Sr.
Senior Pastor | Lighthouse Temple Church, Newark, NJ

ACKNOWLEDGEMENTS

I want to dedicate this book to the following people: The memory of my grandmother, pastor, and Presiding Elder Anna Cooper. You have instilled confidence in me that hell cannot steal. That confidence is in Christ Jesus.

To my mother, Prophet Loria Bracy, who taught me to never settle for less than my best but to strive for more.

To my best friend and love of my life, the lovely Shadae, you are God's gift to me.

To my father in the gospel and pastor, District Elder Mark E. Parrott, Sr., You came into my life right on time. Because of you, I can say, "I've been down in Jesus' name."

To my brother, Deacon Asher Carr: Man, thank you for your expertise, time, assistance, and support. You made it happen, brother! You are going places and will always have my respect.

To the Lighthouse Temple Church of Our Lord Jesus Christ of the Apostolic Faith Inc. I love you all tremendously.

To the photographer, Malcolm Smiley.

CONTENT WARNING

This book contains the following sensitive topics:

Abuse, neglect & abandonment
Anxiety disorders & anxiety attacks
Body shaming
Cheating
Depression
Drug abuse
Mental illness
Panic attacks
Rape
Sexual abuse
Verbal abuse

Some topics may bring up thoughts and emotions that can be overwhelming and should be tackled under the guidance of mental health or other support professionals.

PREFACE

J am passionate about what I do. As a preacher, I am passionate about ministering effectively to the body of Christ and preaching Jesus Christ and HIM crucified to the sinner. I am passionate about writing books that revolutionize the mind, heart, and soul as an author. Also, as a counselor in the mental health profession, I am passionate about getting to the core of mental health issues.

In my senior year of high school, I discovered I was interested in learning the mind. Psychology seemed to be a few of my elective courses that dealt with everyday life issues. I knew that pursuing a career in the mental health profession was one of my endeavors. In 2008, I became more interested in learning about the mind. Now let me be clear. One does not need a psychology degree to understand human behavior. All you need is to be a little street smart. However, knowing what drives that behavior is what I was after.

As I began to study human behavior, I realized that most therapists, psychiatrists, psychologists, and mental health experts were treating the symptoms but not the crux of the issue. In that year, I came across the work of psychologist Dr. Marilyn Sorensen. She specialized in self-esteem. While there are many books on self-worth, her book got to the core of most problems with the human heart: low self-esteem.

It is tragic that very few mental health professionals truly understand the inner expe-

rience of low self-esteem or how to treat this problem. Low self-esteem is not taken seriously either by the general public or the mental health community. Instead, the experience is described as a temporary feeling of inadequacy, a lack of confidence in certain situations, maybe even a negative attitude. However, those who suffer from low self-esteem and are aware that it is the cause of their suffering understand the extent to which it has negatively affected their lives and relationships. Only those with low self-esteem can appreciate the many opportunities lost to their feelings of inadequacy, the heart-wrenching humiliation they have experienced, the overwhelming fear and anxiety they endure, and the magnitude of the hopelessness they have experienced when gripped by this fear (Sorensen, 2-3).

Dr. Sorensen's work in the mental health profession got right to the point. She understood that depression, anxiety, and anger (just to name a few) are not the root but the symptoms of most mental health problems.

She also expounds on the medical component of treating mental health issues: *They also wonder why the medication was recommended so quickly when it was of little value, only serving to mask their anxiety or depression and doing nothing to alter their basic problems (Sorensen, 2).*

I was immediately captivated and on the edge of my seat as I continued to read her work and knew that this woman was on to something that would revolutionize the psychology and psychiatry field. As I started working in the counseling field,

I noticed that mental health issues were not being addressed in this way. There was a reason for this. All licensed clinicians, therapists, psychologists, and psychiatrists must use the *Diagnostic and Statistical Manual of Mental Disorders (DSM-5)*.

For insurance companies to get paid, mental health experts must use the diagnosis already afforded to them in the DSM-5. Since low self-esteem is not treated as a real diagnosis and isn't in the DSM-5 as a primary diagnosis, many are not getting the treatment they need.

> *Unfortunately, an adequate system of maintaining integrity and truth, a system of checks and balances, does not exist in the field of mental health vis-à-vis the validity of the diagnostic manual. Instead, largely because they are a bridge between health practices and insurance coverage, the medical community, which frequently views itself as totally separate from, superior to, or in competition with the mental health community, serves as the primary standard-bearers for deciding both medical and mental health criteria (Sorensen, 123).*

I strongly believe that God doesn't bring us on a new territory to blend in; He brings us on to change the atmosphere. When I began working in the counseling field in 2014, I agreed with Dr. Sorensen that the mental health community was not addressing clients' needs holistically – dealing with low self-worth as the root rather than the symptom. Then the preacher in me received a revelation that wasn't new but biblical.

The Lord Jesus showed me through the scriptures that the issue with low self-esteem is SELF. One of the hardest issues to confront is the issues of self. One of the most intimidating individuals to confront is oneself. The last person we want someone else to confront is ourselves. We live in a self-minded society. Facebook and Instagram selfies. Selfish marriages, selfish friendships, selfish career agendas, and the list goes on and on.

Christ didn't just come to save us from our sin; He also came to save us from ourselves. The Lord Jesus began to show me the difference between self-confidence and Christ-confidence through the word of God. Many of us aren't happy with ourselves because we are trying to esteem ourselves without Christ. Hear me good: There is nothing wrong with knowing our worth and having self-esteem. The problem starts when we put "self" in front of worth. When we prioritize self over esteem the problems multiply.

I wrote this book under the inspiration of the Holy Spirit to many who have battled all their life with self-esteem, never being able to feel the way they desire fully. I wrote this book for those who encourage others but can't seem to believe the pep talk they give themselves when they're alone. I wrote this book to the woman who has battled with either weight, looks or trying to get a man to stay. I wrote this book to the man who defines himself by what he owns, drives, or does for a living.

The Lord Jesus Christ does not want to raise your self-esteem nor give you self-worth. The Lord Jesus wants to be your confidence. I will use the life of David from the Bible to show us some gems and vital truths on being Christ-confident. Jesus wants you Christ-confident. We will see the emotional highs and lows of David's perception of himself and how it affected his thoughts, feelings, and behavior. We will use other Bible characters but solely focus on David. Turn the page and give God your undivided attention.

PART 1

No Confidence
at Home

ONE

I'm Feeling Some Kind of Way

> "Children would rather be from a
> broken home than live in one."
> —Dr. Phillip McGraw

avid had arrived. He is no longer the shepherd boy, the overlooked, or the underrated. He went from being the unsung hero among his family to becoming a king among strangers. Yes, be kind to strangers. We never know who we will bump into again. As the old saying goes, "Be nice to the nerd; he might be your boss someday." How we treat strangers reveals how far we have come from a place called home. In other words, how we treat new people in our lives is an indicator of if we are over the people in our past.

David is now meeting new people. He is talking to kings and sitting in high places. He is no longer the poor boy from Bethlehem and is now the rich King of Israel. Whoever didn't like him couldn't stop this moment. Whoever plotted against him was no match for this moment. The enemies, rumors, manipulation, and family drama failed to keep a good man down. David's steps were ordered by God even when he fell. David was more than a conqueror.

Feeling Out of Place

David wrote that God placed his hands on him (Psalms 139:5). God's hand was on David's life. God had already decided he would go to the palace before his parents decided his name. Nevertheless, success doesn't always taste like success when we have had pain in our mouths. Growing up, David was not always welcomed at home. Living with envious brothers and a father who didn't understand his potential paved the way for insecurities in his life.

Many of us feel out of place in the room with kings, CEOs, and executives by the time we get our foot in the door that Christ has predetermined for us to walk through. We feel guilty for being invited to the big screens, living the blessed life we were not accustomed to growing up. Because David felt out of place at home around his kinfolk, he ended up feeling out of place even in the palace. Yes, the king in his own palace felt out of place.

David is in good company. We all can relate to David. Many of us are trying to adjust to a new life that we feel we don't deserve. We have been out of place so long that when we get in the gate, instead of looking for people to greet, we expect people not to speak. We have been lied to so long at home that we don't trust any compliments in the palace. That expression, "You just don't know how to act," can be applied to David. He wasn't used to royalty; why? He never saw the royalty in himself. **We will never get used to royalty in our lives that we didn't first recognize inside of ourselves.**

> *We will never get used to royalty in our lives that we didn't first recognize inside of ourselves.*

What Does David's House Have
to Do with My House?

The answer is everything. Home is where the heart is. The way we grew up still affects our thoughts, feelings, and behavior even if we aren't aware. Some have had parents that were so verbally abusive that they vowed never to talk to their children in the same way. However, one day in a moment of frustration, after yelling at their kids, they say to themselves, "I sound just like my parents."

Many of us don't see ourselves as healthy functioning adults due to the dysfunctional family we grew up in. While we may be tempted to make excuses for our family, the fact that our family affected our self-esteem (for better or worse) cannot be denied. Some adults are still trying to navigate life, trying hard to do what others consider "normal." Some men attempt to be fathers, although they never heard their father say, "Good job, son." Despite growing up with a cold mother, some women try to be warm to their kids.

Our self-esteem is predicated on our view of ourselves, which begins in childhood. We were not always adults. We came into this world with no guidelines, no identity starter pack, and our parents had no instructions either. They might have raised us while dealing with their low self-esteem. Our perception of ourselves is based on what we were told growing up, what we went through, and how we were treated. Those three components become the lens through which we see the rest of the world.

Encouraged children become encouraged adults. Children who are shown proper affection as children are affectionate adults. Children who are told they are somebody won't have to put other people down to make themselves feel good. On the other hand, if children are ignored when they need attention, they will find it by any means necessary. If they are chastised for having opinions that differ from their mother or father, they will believe their ideas are worthless.

I Need A Minute

David is in the palace, but he doesn't know how to handle it because his parents didn't do "palace talk" with him. Growing up without healthy affirmations will make compliments in our adult lives seem foreign. Have you noticed that some people will discredit you by informing you of their flaws and feelings of inferiority when giving compliments?

They don't mean to. Unfortunately, they have been conditioned to believe the worst about themselves for so long that any compliment that doesn't match their internal "put-downs" will come off like patronizing them or selling a dream.

> *12Saul was afraid of David because the LORD was with David but had left Saul. 13Therefore, Saul sent David away from him and made him commander over a thousand men. David led the troops 14and continued to succeed in all his activities because the LORD was with him. 15When Saul observed that David was very successful, he dreaded him. 16But all Israel and Judah loved David because he led their troops. 17Saul told David, "Here is my oldest daughter Merab. I'll give her to you as a wife if you will be a warrior for me and fight the LORD's battles." But Saul was thinking, "I don't need to raise a hand against him; let the hand*

of the Philistines be against him." ¹⁸ Then David responded, "Who am I, and what is my family or my father's clan in Israel that I should become the king's son-in-law? (1 Samuel 18:12-19, CSB).

God had replaced King Saul, but he is still in a position of power as king. After Saul disobeyed God's orders on two occasions, God had enough. God already had David in mind. However, David's mind was saturated with all his insecurities. He thought low of himself for most of his life that he could not see God in him even in the palace. **Insecurity is at its peak when we can't see Jesus in us.**

Insecurity is at its peak when we can't see Jesus in us.

God has David in the palace, but not to understudy Saul. However, he must learn how to serve someone who didn't know who he is himself. If you study the life of King Saul, he wrestled with insecurities himself (we'll talk about him later. Trust me!) David has insecurity all around him, but he also has a God inside of him. However, David is distracted by thoughts of self-doubt and inferiority that he needs a minute to process that the king wanted to give him his daughter, becoming the king's son-in-law.

What Does David's Kingship Have to Do with Me?

David did not know he was going to be king. He didn't grow up being treated like he would be one. His father, Jesse, did not raise David to be or think like a king. So, by the time he gets into the palace, he is placed over an army of men and offered the king's daughter. He has nothing in his background to compare it with. So, when we are bombarded with thoughts of insecurity and insignificance, those thoughts and bad experiences from our childhood become our only measuring stick and the benchmark we live by.

Many of us were born kings and queens; however, like David, no one or very few people in our family ever pointed out the king or queen in us. Maybe Jesse was never told about the greatness inside of him. Many of us are still upset with our parents for not being there when we were growing up, not showing much affection, encouraging us, or supporting our dreams. **How quickly do children forget that our parents were children before they were parents?**

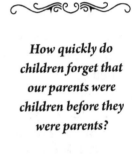

How quickly do children forget that our parents were children before they were parents?

I'm Not Enjoying My Adulthood Because of My Childhood

"I still have marks on my body from my older sister and brother beating me when I was a little girl," said one of my friends one day. She had a heart of gold but couldn't seem to shake childhood wounds in her adulthood. Her wounds were literal. Her wounds wounded her marriage. Her wounds wounded her relationship with her grandchildren. Her childhood wounds made her feel like she was never loved. The scars on her back reminded her of the childhood she so desperately wanted to forget. Unfortunately, she passed away with this burden. **Many times, the parts about our child-**

hood that we hate to revisit, reflect, and reveal are the parts that make us feel insecure. It makes us feel some kind of way.

Many today are still trying to win the approval of their parents at the age of 58, 60, and 70. Many adults feel like their parents never gave them the recognition they wanted. Regardless of how good life may be going for them in their career, educational pursuits, or

> *Many times, the parts about our childhood that we hate to revisit, reflect, and reveal are the parts that make us feel insecure.*

accomplishments, they still want to hear, "I'm proud of you." Others had one parent cheer them on, while the other was a negative critic.

Some grew up with single parents who gave them no encouragement. Others might have had an aunt who believed in them or a cousin who saw their potential. Still, some only had a third-grade teacher or a music teacher who inspired them. Either way, a million people can encourage you, but you still want to hear Mom and Dad say it.

David Knew That His Mother and Father Were Human

David was a writer. Most of his writings were in the book of Psalms. If David had become a published author, his book would have been a bestseller. David wrote about grief, loss, enemies, faith in God, frustration with people, and even the hurt from his family. When it came to his father and mother, he wrote, *When my father and my mother forsake me, then the LORD will take me up (Psalms 27:10).*

From a Hebrew scholarly perspective, this statement made by King David was a proverbial statement. David was not saying that they forsook him; however, he is saying if they were to, he knew he could always count on God. Nevertheless, some adults who read this passage from a western standpoint, take it literally because it is there reality.

When a child cannot say, with confidence, that they know their mother and father will have their back, it leaves a mental paper trail of anxiety, insecurity, and feelings of inferiority. They simply call that "feeling some kind of way." This is why it is so important for children to hear healthy affirmations from their parents to add a sense of worth to their identity. This should be stated at many baby christenings. Dressing up that cute baby in white, taking pictures, and cutting the cake. Still, preachers – please remind the parents that it's not enough to read the Bible to the child and then neglect to give the child healthy affirmations.

Anybody Seen David's Mother?

It has been said that a man's mother is his first girlfriend. A mother teaches her son how to open the door for a woman, talk to a woman, treat a woman, and apologize to a woman. The issue is not that David's father, Jesse, was in the picture; the issue is his mother is not at home. Some men are not wrestling with "daddy issues." Some are battling with "mommy issues." David's father was present but failed to point out the greatness in his son. At the very least, if one parent fails to recognize your gifts and talents, you have the other parent to turn to.

We don't hear about David's mother when Samuel comes to anoint David as the next king of Israel. However, the first time she is mentioned in scripture is when David wants to make sure she is cared for (1 Samuel 22:1). Many children grew up taking care of a parent who has not taken care of them. Keep in mind that in David's day, women were not mentioned unless they played significant roles. We don't know about his relationship with his mother. What we do know is that Jesse did not think his son would be king.

When some children feel like they can't please either parent, that child may look for approval somewhere else, even if they're looking in the direction of a gang, prostitution, or criminal activity. Others may turn their mother and father against each other because that child feels like everyone is against them.

Stressed Parents, Stressed Children

No one knows why David's mother is anonymous in the scriptures. What we do know, from a psycho-theological perspective, is that an absent parent will sometimes create an absence of confidence in a child, sometimes following them up into adulthood. We are not shocked by the number of absent fathers who miss out on their son's games or daughter's recitals. However, a mother who is not there for her children is heavily criticized. Maybe this is how Hagar felt.

> *9-10 One day, Sarah saw the son Hagar the Egyptian had borne to Abraham, poking fun at her son Isaac. She told Abraham, "Get rid of this slave woman and her son. No child of this enslaved person is going to share the inheritance with my son Isaac!" 11-13 The matter gave great pain to Abraham—after all, Ishmael was his son.*

But God spoke to Abraham, "Don't feel bad about the boy and your maid. Do whatever Sarah tells you. Your descendants will come through Isaac. Regarding your maid's son, be assured that I'll also develop a great nation from him—he's your son, too." [14-16] *Abraham got up early the next morning, got some food together and a canteen of water for Hagar, put them on her back, and sent her away with the child. She wandered off into the desert of Beersheba. When the water was gone, she left the child under a shrub and went off, fifty yards or so. She said, "I can't watch my son die." As she sat, she broke into sobs. (Genesis 21:9-16, MSG).*

I can only imagine how difficult this mother's situation was. It has been said that if being a mother was easy, being a father would be, too. Let's take a minute and examine her self-esteem. Her childhood dreams were crushed. What little girl wants to grow up to be a maid? She was working for a rich couple but is still a slave. She was not a babysitter or nanny. They got paid. She was enslaved. Her boss was her baby's daddy, and her boss's wife (the one who suggested Abraham sleep with her to impregnate her) suddenly wants to put her son out. Her self-esteem as a woman must have been in the basement.

At least some women have a job or two, can support themselves, and can brag, "I don't depend on no man." Hagar had no bragging rights. She was so devastated and hurt by looking at her son, who she felt helpless and hopeless to help, lose his future over her petty boss's inflated ego. She walked away from the child because she just couldn't stand the sight of it. Not everyone walks away from us because they want to.

Some walk away because it hurts to stay, knowing they don't have the resources to help. And let's not forget the only thing she received for child support from her baby daddy is a loaf of bread and a canteen of water.

Interestingly, I read a statistic by a psychologist that stated that one million people call out of work due to stress. That part may sound like, "Tell people what else is new. We know that already." The interesting thing is that psychologists reported that most stress is connected to not forgiving oneself for past mistakes. Furthermore, CNN reported years ago that twenty-five percent of our behavior is driven by guilt from the past. Can you imagine Hagar's stress as an enslaved person and mother who was fired from her job and has a mouth to feed while barely feeding herself?

Many of our children are stressed out because they have stressed-out parents who don't have the proper coping skills. Some parents are yelling at their children as soon as they get in from work, not because their children have done anything wrong, but because the kids are an easy target. Some kids fall asleep in school because they're up all night after being awakened by their parents arguing at three in the morning. Some girl in high school is struggling while on the honor roll because her stressed-out father molested her.

Hagar did not cuss her son out in her distress, nor did she keep him up all night. She didn't even tell him, "You are the man of the house now." She had no house to call home. She did what comes off selfish to many: she left him. Nevertheless, God loves the children. Hagar's baby started to cry, and God did not ask for him to hush, but God wanted Hagar to listen:

> *17-18 Meanwhile, God heard the boy crying. The angel of God called from Heaven*

to Hagar, "What's wrong, Hagar? Don't be afraid. God has heard the boy and knows the fix he's in. Up now; get the boy. Hold him tight. I'm going to make of him a great nation." 19 Just then, God opened her eyes. She looked. She saw a well of water. She went to it and filled her canteen and gave the boy a long, cool drink.20-21 God was on the boy's side as he grew up. He lived out in the desert and became a skilled archer. He lived in the Paran wilderness. And his mother got him a wife from Egypt. (Genesis 21:17-21, MSG).

God heard the boy's cry where he was and told Hagar to get him. I want to tell that parent in a custody battle right now to get your child. Don't allow the "beef" between you and your kid's mother or kid's father to interfere with the love of the child or children. They did not ask to be here. They need to see love – not another wrestling or shouting match.

Where's My Drink?

Notice Hagar quenches her son's thirst with the water God gave her, but where is her water? Parents wrestle with insecurities every day that children don't realize. The effects of the divorce have made that mother feel like she isn't beautiful while raising her daughter to think she is beautiful. So instead of encouraging her daughter, she tells her that all men cheat, "don't trust them," and the daughter is thirsty as a grown woman. Insecurity will leave a negative legacy in the family.

Jesus Christ referred to the Holy Ghost as "living water" (John 7:38). Many of us are depleted of love, encouragement, resources, income, esteem, worth, and dreams because we spent all our lives giving it away. For every adult that's still thirsty from a drained childhood of parched esteem, I encourage you to come to Jesus. He is a fountain of living water. Don't spend your adulthood going to the wrong person, career, group, or materialism to quench your thirst. There are many areas of our lives, even as adults, that are dry because of the insecurities in our childhood.

However, I want you to know that the Lord Jesus Christ is water in dry places. Why remain a parched victim when we can be hydrated victors?

My Dad Never Left, but He Left Me Out

"4 So Samuel did as the LORD instructed. When he arrived at Bethlehem, the town elders came trembling to meet him. "What's wrong?" they asked. "Do you come in peace?"5 "Yes," Samuel replied. "I have come to sacrifice to the LORD. Purify yourselves and come with me to the sacrifice." Then Samuel performed the purification rite for Jesse and his sons and invited them to the sacrifice, too.6 When they arrived, Samuel took one look at Eliab. He thought, "Surely this is the LORD's anointed!" 7 But the LORD said to Samuel, "Don't judge by his appearance or height, for I have rejected him. The LORD doesn't see things the way you see them. People judge by outward appearance, but the LORD looks at the heart."8 Then Jesse told his son Abinadab to step forward and walk in front of Samuel.

But Samuel said, "This is not the one the LORD has chosen." ⁹ Next, Jesse summoned Shimea,[a] but Samuel said, "Neither is this the one the LORD has chosen." ¹⁰ In the same way, all seven of Jesse's sons were presented to Samuel. But Samuel said to Jesse, "The LORD has not chosen any of these." ¹¹ Then Samuel asked, "Are these all the sons you have?" "There is still the youngest," Jesse replied. "But he's out in the fields watching the sheep and goats." "Send for him at once," Samuel said. "We will not sit down to eat until he arrives." (1 Samuel 16:4-11, NLT).

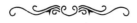

His father was present in the house, but he did not summon his son.

Do you know how we feel when our friends go out without inviting us? As humans, we hate being the last to know or not being invited. It is a special kind of adrenaline rush not to be invited. Still, we have to see the pictures posted on Facebook alone at home. David was the youngest, the overlooked, and unacknowledged. **His father was present in the house, but he did not summon his son.** Many of our children do not return home because they are not called.

It's a hard fight to stay where you felt you never mentally belonged physically. Many of us grew up to be loners because we always felt alone at the dinner table, cookout, family reunion, or Christmas family get-together. Jesse might have loved David but never thought highly of him.

It's a hard fight to stay where you felt you never mentally belonged physically.

Jesse gave him a house to live in but not a home to feel he belonged in. David had all types of idiosyncrasies that came off as an oddity to his family. Still, he was different and wonderfully made in the eyes of God. Jesus Christ wants to remind you of those unique qualities that you have. He gave them to you. Christ is not taking them back. Regardless of who in your family called you arrogant, weird, stuck up, or didn't understand you, stay different. God created many masterpieces, and you are one of them. AND DON'T YOU FORGET THAT.

A Daddy's Girl Who Is Her Mother's Daughter

I love documentaries on famous actors, singers, and more. I also love when the main character narrates their own story. I remember Natalie Cole narrating a documentary. Natalie was a gifted singer with a sound of her own. One thing was clear in her movie: she was a daddy's girl. She loved her father, the famous Nat King Cole. She spends time talking about how much she loved her father and their connection in a segment. Mr. Cole was calm, cool, and collected. He was easy to talk to and easy for his daughter to love.

Before her father died of lung cancer, little Natalie was upset that her mother, Maria Cole, didn't tell her how sick her father was. You see, Mrs. Cole had a different demeanor and a confusing way of handling things. According to Natalie, her mother was not the type to cry and express emotion. She dealt with sadness, situations, and sickness with denial, acting as if everything was ok. That coping mechanism was not good for Natalie's self-esteem. She had confidence from her father but insecurity from her mother.

Many of our women today love their fathers but have a "nice-nasty" or toxic relationship with their mothers. When two women are alike in the same house, they do not always get along. This was the case with Natalie and her mother. Her songs won everyone's approval to accept her mother. Even though Natalie's father passed away when she was a young girl, she knew she had his approval. On the other hand, her mother lived to see Natalie become a woman but did not respect her daughter.

It is human nature to reach out to the emotionally unavailable or absent parent than the one who stayed. Natalie is grieving the father who died and grieving the living mother. It's a slow living death to feel like your parents don't approve of who you are, in God, regardless of what you do.

Approval Addict

Long after her father's death, Natalie found out that heroin could numb her pain. She wasn't raised to be that way, but she was old enough to make her own decisions. Don't count the silky singer out just yet, as she recovers from heroin. However, Natalie's first addiction was still on the rise. She was an approval addict – still trying to win her mother's accolades. Maria Cole was not easily impressed. She loved her daughter but had a strange way of showing it, as the movie portrays. She wanted the best for her daughter, as any mother would, but Natalie had a different perception.

Natalie isn't the only approval addict. Many of us are trying so desperately to win the approval of others who may never approve. Many of us have climbed the ladder of success but still feel as if the ones we love don't notice. At the heart of most approval addicts is the need for attention. Parents need to teach their kids that not everyone will approve of them.

However, how can the parents teach that if they struggle with it themselves, like in Maria Cole's case?

Mom, This Parenting Style Isn't Working

I can remember as a child, when my mother would yell at me, I had a scripture ready for her (laughing out loud). I would quote, "Provoke not children to wrath" (Ephesians 6:4). Funny, but true. The same Bible that teaches children to honor their parents also teaches parents not to provoke their children to anger. Why must parents not provoke their children to anger? The Bible gives us an answer: "Fathers, provoke not your children to anger, lest they be discouraged" (Colossians 3:21). Many children with anger problems are really discouraged.

A discouraged child is one who is easily sensitive to rejection, disapproval, criticism and can often be too open to anyone who shows them approval. Natalie was discouraged by her mother, and feeling discouraged early sets the stage for insecurity to be the wrong tag-a-long and her partner to succeed. Natalie couldn't seem to enjoy her success the way she desired due to her choices, decisions, and lingering insecurity from a mother she could not please. Children are more easily discouraged than they have ever been before. Since children are a gift from the Lord Jesus, ask Him to assist you with the child He gave you.

She Said She Would Always Love You but Didn't Love Herself

I can remember that Saturday night like yesterday. I was coming home hearing that Whitney Houston was gone. Her death touched the hearts of many just as much as her voice. Whitney was known for her famous song, "I Will Always Love You." As much exuberance as she brought to herself, it appeared that she didn't see herself in a positive light. When she passed away in 2012, some of her close friends reported that they felt Whitney did not love herself.

Many parents have done the best they possibly could to love their children while secretly fighting to love themselves. One father expressed that "when my son looks at me, he is looking at a failure." This statement was made by a father that was still beating himself up for not having a good job, not being where he wanted to be in life, and giving in to bouts of drug and alcohol addiction.

I want to encourage every parent struggling with feelings of guilt and shame for the mistakes you believe you have made that placed your child or children in jeopardy to forgive yourself. Maybe you have battled with addiction, and despite your multiple apologies, your children are still being mean to you because of the bitterness they carry inside for you. It may take a while for them to forgive you. Some of them won't. However, you must forgive yourself while waiting on your family too.

I Was Raised Right, but I Still Feel Wrong

One of the myths and stereotypes of drug and alcohol addiction is assuming that all addicts were brought up in a bad home, grew up in poverty, or didn't want anything out of life. This is so far from the truth. Many who grew up in good homes, Christian households, were taught good manners, lived in good neighborhoods, and had to be in the house by the time the streetlights came on, but still went the wrong way. What is the problem?

The problem is that they grew up feeling terrible about themselves based on their internal perception. Whitney was raised in a good Christian home with a God-fearing mother and wonderful family but still couldn't seem to shake that "not good enough feeling." Where does this feeling emanate from? The answer is our thoughts. Each of us has unwanted memories we wish we could forget. Each of us has to wake up every day and fight thoughts of discouragement. Each of us has thoughts that try to make us doubt who we are in the eyes of the Lord Jesus Christ. The Bible puts it this way: "As a man thinketh in his heart, so is he" (Proverbs 23:7).

We often ask people how their love life is. However, one's love life will never supersede one's thought life. How we view ourselves affects even the good things or people in our lives that Christ has sent if we view ourselves in a negative light. Many of you reading this book have greatness inside of you. You grew up being told you can make it and have succeeded and continue to excel in many areas of your life, but are harassed by thoughts in your mind telling you that you aren't worth it.

Our feelings follow our thoughts. I can't tell a person, "Don't feel that way." People don't want to feel bad about themselves on purpose. What we can encourage others not to do is not think that way. What we go through in life can look worse than if we look at ourselves negatively. I challenge you to stop changing people; change how you negatively see yourself in the Lord Jesus. That will help you deal with difficult people who won't change even though they can.

David Wasn't Trained To Be King, but He Was Anointed To Be One

The word of God advises parents to "train up a child in the way he should go: and when he is old, he will not depart from it" (Proverbs 22:6). Jesse, however, did not train David to be a king. He only trained David to be a son, shepherd, and man. Give Jesse some credit, though. How could he train his son to be a king when God didn't tell him when David was born? How could he train his son to be a king when Jesse was not a king himself? David's upbringing shows us three things.

1. **Many parents never trained us to be who God wanted us to be because God didn't tell them.** Nobody can keep a secret like our Father in heaven. God didn't reveal that David would be king until Samuel came to the house to anoint him. God will often place us in families or circles that don't know our purpose so that we can be dependent on Christ for direction. Your family may know your "ways" and behavior, but it is Christ Jesus the Lord who knows the reason behind your ways. Forgive your parents for not knowing what God did not tell them. Jesse found out David would be king when David found out.

2. **What happened or didn't happen in your house won't stop the anointing from getting to your house.** David was overlooked, mistreated, rejected, and looked down on by the people in his house. However, none of those atrocities could keep the oil of the anointing of God from finding David's address. See, the enemy (Satan) knows that God has predestined you from the foundation of the world. The devil knows that he cannot stop what Christ has already planned to do in your life. So, Satan starts really early in our childhood to make us doubt who Christ says we are and will be. The anointing of the Holy Ghost does not need a GPS to find you. Your childhood will not cancel out what God has in

store for your future. In fact, "eyes have not seen, nor ear heard, neither have entered into the heart of man, the things which God hath prepared for them that love him" (1 Corinthians 2:9).

3. **God has more for you than where you grew up.** Many of us are loyal to where we have been because we don't know where Christ will take us. Others are loyal to where they have been because they think Christ has no other venues for them. Some have been manipulated into staying home by the people they love simply because they are afraid of succeeding. Still, others are loyal to where they were because they have been tricked into believing there is no other place for them outside of the home.

Notice, Proverbs 22:6 says children are to be trained in the way they should *go*. In other words, parents are to train their children to leave the nest. However, if Jesse does not train his son to be king, he at least must train him to go wherever Christ sends him. Many who grew up with you have been jealous of you, degraded you, mistreated you, and even left you out. Still, David proves that the anointing of God loves the black sheep of the family.

Through Jesus Christ, I challenge you not to be a victim. Don't allow thoughts of insecurity to make you feel sorry for yourself. Forgive them so that you can move on and into your prepared place. Don't fear new places because God will always have someone to assist you. Even David kept on living until he was able to say with confidence, "Surely goodness and mercy shall follow me all the days of my life: and I will dwell in the house of the LORD forever" (Psalms 23:6).

TWO

The Fear of Being Me

"God is not trying to make you a better person;
Christ wants to make you like Him."
—Dr. Matthew L. Stevenson

"I've been thinking about killing myself." Those are the last words any good mother or father wants to hear their children say. No good husband wants to come home and see his wife holding a razor blade to her wrist when he walks into her bedroom. The suicide of a loved one, especially witnessing it with one's own eyes, can traumatize someone for the rest of their lives if they let it.

However, if you want to know what a living suicide is, ask yourself one question: **Is the life I am living the life I want, or is it the life others have decided for me?** It has been said, "if you don't know who you are, anyone can fool you, rule you, and control you." I would submit to you that the only feeling worse than not knowing who you are at this stage in the game is to know

Is the life I am living the life I want, or is it the life others have decided for me?

who you are in Christ and not live up to it. That's a living suicide. It is a mental health phenomenon and daily torture. While fooling the world, our families, spouses, "side-chicks," "boy-toys," and everyone we are trying to impress, we cannot run from the purpose and will of God on the inside of us. I'm not addressing the fear of spiders, closed spaces, fear of loss, or fear of being left behind.

I'm talking about the risk of being who we are and relinquishing our desire to please others. I'm talking about waking up one day, having the epiphany hit you in the face that the life you're living is not yours. From your wardrobe to your college degree to your career path – it has all been under the spotlight of people we admire or love dearly.

Forbidden Fruit or Insecure Fruit?

Now, the serpent was more cunning than any animal of the field which the LORD God had made. And he said to the woman, "Has God said, 'You shall not eat from any tree of the garden'?" 2 The woman said to the serpent, "From the fruit of the trees of the garden we may eat; 3 but from the fruit of the tree which is in the middle of the garden, God has said, 'You shall not eat from it or touch it, or you will die.'"4 The serpent said to the woman, "You certainly will not die! 5 For God knows that on the day you eat from it your eyes will be opened, and you will [a]become like God, knowing good and evil." 6 When the woman saw that the tree was good for food, that it was a delight to the eyes, and that the tree was desirable to make one wise, she took some of its fruit and ate. She also gave some to her husband with her, and he ate. ⁷ Then the eyes of both of them were opened. They knew that they were naked, and they sewed fig leaves together and made themselves waist coverings. ⁸ Now, they heard the sound of the LORD God walking in the garden in the cool of the day, and the man and his wife hid from the presence of the LORD God among the trees of the garden. ⁹ Then the LORD God called to the man and said to him, "Where are you?" ¹⁰ He said, "I heard the sound of You in the garden, and I was afraid because I was naked; so I hid." ¹¹ And He said, "Who told you that you were naked? Have you eaten from the tree from which I commanded you not to eat? (Genesis 3:1-11, NASB).

Who in their right mind doesn't want what they cannot have? It is embedded in our flesh.

Most of us know the Adam and Eve story. Eve ate the forbidden fruit and gave it to her husband. However, I want to show you some hidden gems often overlooked in the dialogue between the serpent (Satan) and Eve that set the stage for insecurity:

- **Satan used the word of God to make Eve think she was lacking.** Eve was a complete woman who needed nothing outside of God's purpose for her life to fulfill her. Eve was Christ-confident. The problem was that

Eve allowed the serpent to talk her into believing that she was less of a woman without the forbidden fruit. Could it be possible that you are holding on to or who Christ told you to let go of because you think you're lacking without it or them? God promised us that he would withhold no good thing from those who walk uprightly before him (Psalms 84:11).

- **The fruit was forbidden because they did not need it.** God purposely placed a tree in the garden that they did not need to teach them how to live with what they could not have. When we want a new start from a bad relationship, many of us will often delete the text thread or pictures from our phones. In drug and alcohol recovery, clients are cautioned not to go into areas that can trigger a relapse. Running every time something or someone gives us a sense of inferiority will create a cycle of avoiding the unavoidable to relieve our anxiety.

- **After eating the forbidden fruit, they went from being Christ-conscious to self-conscious.** Before Eve ate the fruit, she talked about what God said. If you want to know how you feel about yourself, see yourself, think about yourself, listen to what you tell yourself. Jesus Christ never taught self-esteem; he taught Christ-esteem (we will discuss that in further detail later. Don't rush). Once they ate the forbidden fruit, guilt and shame walked into their life. Low self-esteem is not low self-esteem without guilt and shame. Guilt is about the past. Shame is one's perception of themselves after what happened in the past. Guilt is feeling insignificant because of what one did in the past. Shame is having a faulty view of oneself because of what one did.

- **"The lust of the flesh, the lust of the eyes, and the pride of life" (1 John 2:15-16) are Satan's main tools to set us up for insecurity.** The above passage shows us that when the woman "saw that the tree was good for food" (the lust of the flesh), "a delight to the eyes" (the lust of the eye), and "the tree was desirable to make one wise" (the pride of the life) Eve ate the forbidden fruit and gave it to her husband.

The lust of the flesh alludes to things we think will satisfy us that aren't pleasing to God and is out of his will for our lives. We feel that without this, we can't get through the night. The lust of the eyes adds insult to the injury from the lust of the flesh. The lust of the eyes takes its course when we begin to desire things that we only want because it's in view. If we had never seen it, we would not have desired it. The real killer is the pride of life. The forbidden thing we think we want is the thing we only desire because we believe it adds value to our false sense of self and lack of confidence. Let me place these principles in a scenario.

In the 2009 film, *Obsessed,* Derek Charles, played by Idris Elba, is married to Sharon Charles, played by Beyonce. They are a successful couple enjoying the good life, with no distractions, until Lisa Sheridan shows up for work. Lisa is an office temp who gets hired on short notice. Derek was not aware until he got to the office one day. Sharon is shocked when Derek reveals to her later that he has a female secretary while discussing how their day went. Sharon reminds him that she thought they both agreed on no female secretaries.

Derek is a faithful guy. He never cheats on Sharon, not one time in this film. The problem was that he kept it a secret from his wife that he was being sexually harassed by this woman who was obsessed with him. However, if you will allow me to put my therapy cap on for a moment, this woman's obsession was rooted in how she took rejection. She was already attracted to Charles, but there is a scene where she is crying over her marriage in the lunchroom, and Derek comes in to encourage her.

He reminds her that she is a beautiful woman, and any man would be lucky to have her. As innocent as that sounded, it catered to her need for affirmation, making her feel good about her insecurities. Derek made her feel confident and desirable with one comment. That made him even more desirable to her. Boom! The lust of the flesh is ignited through his affirmations to her self-worth. The lust of the eyes is on 24-hour surveillance as she watches him daily at work, contemplating her next move to seduce him. The pride of life was born when she placed something in his drink to sleep with him.

Notice the similarity between Lisa and Eve in the garden. The serpent spoke to Eve's sense of worth, making her think that without the forbidden fruit, she won't be like God, knowing as much as God knows. Derek spoke to Lisa's insecurity, making her think that ANY man could be her man. Eve could not eat from ANY tree in the garden, and Lisa was not meant to have ANY man. Dr. Jamal Harrison Bryant put it this way: "Confidence is not just about accepting who you are. It's also about accepting who you're not." In Eve's moments of insecurity, she feared that she wasn't complete without the forbidden fruit.

What makes an individual go after those married or in a relationship? Sometimes it's just plain old attraction. Other times, it's infatuation. However, at the core is the fear of starting over. Some may not want to put in the effort of finding and opening up to someone they know. Others may feel that no one will ever stay with them long enough. One of my friends once said to me, "I don't have a problem getting a man; I have problems keeping one." As we continued to explore the core issue of her relational battles, she understood that some men just leave simply because they never planned on staying. The challenge is not to prove our worth by making others stay.

You Don't Get to Pick Your Fruit

I don't know how you are, but I don't like to lose. It takes a while for us to understand that everyone who came into our lives did not come to stay. Many are battling feelings of inferiority because they have rated themselves on what and who they lost. Others have endured so many losses that they refuse to try again. Then some are what I call "stubbornly hurt."

Stubbornly hurt means, "Since I can't make you stay, I will try to stop you from leaving." This is what we call a fatal attraction. Many women felt if they proved that they were wife material, the man would stay. Some men thought she would never look at another man if he put enough money on the table. We cannot control who stays or goes. We can only be the best version of ourselves that Christ has called us to be and accept that it is their loss.

Let me tell you about Ramon. He was a taxi driver, who gave a ride to a woman, who we will call Latrice. They had a small talk in the car, but they both liked the conversation and exchanged numbers. They both began to spend time together until Latrice decided she would slow things down one day. There's nothing wrong with that, right? Not if you ask Ramon. He was used to his exes either slowing the pace down or leaving him. In the past, he would cry about it. This time, he decided to deal with his insecurities that fueled his fears in a more "nice-nasty" way.

Ramon began to play sick to manipulate Latrice to come and spend time with him. Feeling like he was lucky for a woman like her to take an interest in him in the first place, he became indirectly controlling to make sure he knew her every move. Knowing women don't like controlling men, he gave clever reasons for coming off controlling. He said things like, "I love having you around," and "I don't know what I would do if you were out of my sight." She knew better but felt sorry for him.

She explained that things were not working out between them because he was too controlling. She expressed that she only entertained him because she was going through a breakup, and he was a nice man. Ramon was devastated – not only because she broke off the relationship, but because she confirmed what he secretly believed: that he wasn't worthy of love from beautiful women.

Ramon's fear and anxiety were deeply rooted in unhealthy self-esteem that caused him to act in desperate ways that destroyed the very thing he wanted to keep: his relationship. Fear and anxiety stem from a belief that one is inadequate without someone or something special.

Ramon began having flashbacks of all the women who rejected him in the past, blaming them for his unhappiness. He was not aware that his belief in unworthiness caused him to behave in ways that turned women off in the past. His insecurities were destroying the good fruit in his life.

I am the Real Vine, and my Father is the Farmer. He cuts off every branch of me that doesn't bear grapes. And every grape-bear-

ing branch prunes back so it will bear even more. You are already pruned back by the message I have spoken (John 15:1-3, MSG).

There are a few things to take away from Jesus' statement above. First, notice even the good branches get cut back. It's one thing to cut branches due to bad fruit. That is understandable. However, many of us have toxic people in our lives that we tolerate out of fear and anxiety. The fear behind tolerating toxic individuals is the anxiety of starting over after letting them go. Furthermore, it's the fear that losing them will confirm our perception of ourselves that we used them to cover up.

Let's get back to the good fruit. Jesus informs us that even good fruit has to get cut. The truth is that we can be a good tree, produce good fruit, and lose it. That does not make us feel good. I'm afraid that the pulpit is overlooking these parts of scripture. We teach about God adding but negate that the same Jesus who adds will also subtract. We are not telling people that they can be a good branch, connected to a good vine (Jesus Christ), and still lose fruit.

We often define God's love based on addition. If God gives us more, we think we must be worthwhile individuals. Nevertheless, I would like you to know that it's not safe to trust a God who adds but doesn't subtract from us. Jesus Christ, the Lord, loves us too much to allow excess junk to stay in our lives that are hindering where he will take us. Next, Christ tells the disciples in the above passage that he cleans the fruit through his words.

Because of Christ's word over our lives, not everyone will stay in

Because of Christ's word over our lives, not everyone will stay in our lives.

our lives. Can I tell you that a real word from God will not make everyone stay; it will make many leave.

If "It's Their Loss," Why Does It Hurt So Bad?

I often say that if we don't know who we are on a good day, it will be hard to get through life on a bad day. I have come to understand that it is not what they did to us that hurts, as it is how we see ourselves in the face of the hurt. If we already think small of ourselves, we have already subconsciously taught ourselves to magnify the identity of those who have hurt us. Let's face it: getting hurt hurts. However, the hurt hurts differently when we already have an unhealthy view of ourselves.

Most of us have heard the phrase, "It's their loss." This is normally said to cheer us up about the rejection, abandonment, and betrayals in our lives. While phrases like that make us feel like we are not alone, it doesn't always change its feeling. If we "are a good catch," "have a lot to offer," and "anyone would be glad to have us," why does it hurt so bad? I can offer you a few reasons.

For one, sometimes we just don't want to accept that some people are not for us. We might have had good times with them. We might have cried with them or even made love to them. However, they are just not for us. Secondly, some individuals use manipulation to believe we cannot make it without them. They caught us at a bad time in our lives when our thoughts about ourselves did not reflect God's thoughts about us. Guilt is a powerful tactic that causes us to stay with the toxicity of the wrong people one day too long.

Deep down inside, you know this person is not good for you, and they stress you out. Even your close friends and family have brought this to your attention. Still, it's hard to let go of those who have us dependent on them for approval and validation. Furthermore, I want you to know that you should never let anyone use guilt to get another free pass in your life. Now let's get down to the real reason: The "God-reason."

Notice in the above passage that we read, in John 15:1-3 MSG, Christ Jesus is the one who cuts the good branches back. The question is, why would Christ cut good branches that are producing good fruit? Why would he take away people who made us feel good about ourselves? Why would the Lord Jesus allow a job that I love to let me go? A job that provided more income than the two jobs I was working before? The answer is simple: because of His word in our life.

> *10 The rain and snow come down from the heavens and stay on the ground to water the earth. They cause the grain to grow, producing seed for the farmer and bread for the hungry. 11 It is the same with my word I send it out, and it always produces fruit. It will accomplish all I want it to, and it will prosper everywhere I send it (Isaiah 55:10-11, NLT).*

Did you notice that the Lord makes it clear that the fruit comes from His word? That's good news! Regardless of the fruit, you lose, the source is the word of God. Hear when I tell you, the challenge is not to base your faith on the fruit God cuts back, but the word of God. Even the Bible says, *the grass withers, the flower fades, but the word of our God will stand forever (Isaiah 40:8, ESV).* There used to be an old song that said, "You've been waiting on deliverance. It seems it just won't come. Body sick. Pain everywhere. It seems nobody cares. The devil is a liar and a deceiver too. God is not through blessing you."

The Main Fears That Come After Us

1. The Fear of People Seeing Us for Who We Are

Everything gets screenshotted now. Many are even afraid to run for office due to fear and anxiety of leaked videos. Many of us have spent years perfecting our masks so that the people we are trying to impress don't know the real us.

It takes confidence in Christ to hold your head up after your mistakes. All it takes is a little fear and insecurity to cover it up. Others are not battling secrets. Some are simply trying to live up to the name others have given them while growing up. Some children were praised so much for their achievements on getting honor roll, winning spelling bees, and being so talented that they criticize themselves when they don't win first place in the game we call life. Someone in the family labeled you "the strongest one in the family," and at fifty-two, you're still trying to be strong for people instead of letting them find their own strength. Or your problem may be that you were confident at one point. However, you shared your goals and dreams with those who shot you down with negativity, projecting their fears onto you.

They have never seen or heard of that kind of success in the family (even though they secretly want it), so they encourage you to stay in your place. Some people in our lives, namely the people we love most and are dear to us, mean well. However, they evaluate us based on their feelings of unworthiness.

Lastly, the issue for your insecurities lies in the fact that you're spending so much time, effort, and money trying to prove that you are capable that it's increasing the anxiety of your insecurities. Don't you know one of the greatest traits of freedom is having nothing to prove? On the other hand, some of you may be trying to prove that you aren't who they say you are. Stop trying to change someone's mind about you, even if it's your husband. We can't stop people from thinking just like we can't stop them from talking.

Christ-Confidence vs. Self-Confidence

Right now, I want to pause and show you some differences between Christ-confidence and self-confidence related to the fear of having flaws exposed. Self-confidence is always trying to fight its own battle. To be self-confident is to be self-reliant. Jesus Christ hated that. Did I just use Christ and hate in the same sentence? Absolutely! It's in the word.

Jesus said, "If any man comes to me, and *hate* not his father, and mother, and wife, and children, and brethren, and sisters, yea and *his own life* also, he *can not* be my disciple" (Luke 14:26).

What is Jesus Christ talking about? Is He telling us to hate our family and ourselves? No. The word hate in this context means to prefer ourselves and our family over Christ – Jesus does not want this. In other words, Christ is telling us to follow Him. We have to choose to be Christ-confident over self-confident. Matthew's gospel put it this way:

"If any man will come after me, let him *deny himself*, and take up his cross, and follow me" (Matthew 16:24).

Getting into the kingdom of Christ is all about giving up your self-confidence for his confidence (which is one of the best decisions I have ever made). Remember when I said earlier that self-confidence likes to fight its own battles? Self-confidence relies too much on SELF to deal with naysayers, secrets, approval, mistakes, and the fear of being exposed. Hear me good when I say that Christ loves fighting our battles. You don't have to face your secrets alone. You don't have to live in fear of being exposed by people sitting on the past themselves.

> *Lift up your heads, O ye gates; and be ye lift up, and ye everlasting doors; and the king of glory shall come in. Who is the King of glory? The LORD strong and mighty, the LORD mighty in battle (Psalms 24:7-8).*

When we have Christ-esteem, we will not entertain thoughts of inadequacy. Christ-confident individuals aren't going to continue to let thoughts of what could go wrong keep them from doing what's right. They have a confidence that only the Holy Ghost can give that says, *I can do all things through Christ that strengthens me (Philippians 4:13).*

Furthermore, Christ-confident saints will not act like what they said about our past sins and mistakes were not true. We just refuse to live there any longer. The Bible says, *We are new creatures in Christ (2 Corinthians 5:17).* Even if we backslide since we were saved, we obey the conviction of the Holy Spirit, repent, and move on. We admit, quit, and forget it.

Christ-confident saints live on what the Bible and the Lord Jesus Christ says about us through the comfort of the Holy Ghost. We don't even live by what we think about ourselves.

We Have the Mind of Christ, According to Philippians 2:5

2. The Fear of Rejection After Revealing Our True Selves

No matter how close you think you are with your loved ones, there is always something you or they aren't telling you.

You may object and even say, "I tell my spouse everything!" I've seen guarded individuals say, "I'm an open book." A friend of mine used to say, "I talk a lot, making people think I'm telling them all my business." People simply tell us what they want us to know. Now let's be clear, we all have things about ourselves that we keep private that are not necessarily negative. However, there's a difference between secrecy and privacy.

Many don't keep secrets to be evil or manipulative. Many keep secrets out of fear that if they reveal their insecurities, the people they love might see them differently. It's like the girl whose family considers her a tomboy because she doesn't carry a purse and likes to play with boys. The last thing her mother is thinking is that her daughter may be gay. This girl loves her mom to death, but she knows her mother is a strong Bible-believing Christian.

The daughter is not saved, but she loves her mother. She fears her mother will disown her for being on the downlow. Now let me footnote that lesbianism and homosexuality are abominations in the sight of God. It is a sin (1 Corinthians 6:9-11). Nevertheless, a parent must continue to show love to their children even if they are on the down-low or have already come out of the closet. The Bible encourages parents to influence their children by their godly lifestyle (1 Corinthians 7:14-15).

You don't have to be on the down-low to have secrets. One of the cornerstone vices of unhealthy self-esteem is the fear of revealing one's thoughts and feelings of inferiority to the people we want to look at us in a positive light. Many of us cannot enjoy the people Christ sent into our lives because we are spending an immense amount of time trying to figure out why they're with you, why they love you, and hoping they don't get tired of you. Even if we don't verbalize these statements to them, they remain unsecured in the seat of our soul.

Succeeding With Insecurities

Have you ever wondered how the most gifted people can feel so insecure? Have you noticed the lightweight who self-consciously believes they're overweight? Or it could be the professional who can run a business as you've never seen but can't seem to shake that inadequate feeling. How can we be highly successful, gifted, anointed, and talented in one or various areas of our lives but battle with insecurities simultaneously?

Speaking from the counselor's desk, let me clarify this ongoing phenomenon. Many often assume that low self-esteem and success can't live together, but clinically speaking, it happens every day. It is psychologically possible to be insecure about gifted and great things. As Dr. Marilyn Sorensen states in *Breaking the Chains of Low Self-esteem*, "Many people who have extremely low self-esteem are achieving at high levels in their careers."

David was good at war. The Bible backs up David's accomplishments. David succeeded in any assignment that God afforded him. Nevertheless, the soon-to-be king couldn't see why people made a big deal out of him. He didn't understand why others loved him. Then we find out why David thinks so low of himself when King Saul offers him his daughter:

> *14 David continued to succeed in everything he did, for the LORD was with him. 15 When Saul recognized this, he became even more afraid of him. 16 But all Israel and Judah*

loved David because he successfully led his troops into battle.[17] One day, Saul said to David, "I am ready to give you my older daughter, Merab, as your wife. But first, you must prove yourself to be a real warrior by fighting the LORD's battles." For Saul thought, "I'll send him out against the Philistines and let them kill him rather than doing it myself."[18] "Who am I, and what is my family in Israel that I should be the king's son-in-law?" David exclaimed. "My father's family is nothing!"[19] So[a] when the time came for Saul to give his daughter Merab in marriage to David, he gave her instead to Adriel, a man from Meholah.(1 Samuel 18:14-19, NLT).

Notice a few things in the above passage. David's success was connected to the presence of the LORD being with him. Yes, God can be with us, and we can still feel insecure. You can be spirit-filled and doubt your calling. You can be a prophet with a real prediction in your mouth from God, yet you wonder why you can't predict when secret insecurities will go away. Now pause. David commented that *In thy presence is fullness of joy; at thy right hand, there are pleasures always (Psalms 16:11).*

Wait a minute, David! You mean to tell me you are in the presence of the LORD, enjoying his pleasures, and feel insecure? That is very true. Furthermore, let me also flip this and say that maybe David came into the joy of God's presence to polish his confidence in God. What am I saying? I am saying that David was Christ-confident. David put it this way:

God is the strength of my life (Psalms 27:1).

Secondly, people loved David on a level he struggled to love himself. Some wives can't see past their insecurities to see what their husbands see in them. Some husbands get paranoid when another man they deem to be better looking speaks to their wife because they believe she is only with him for money. I want you to develop the discipline to let others love you.

Lastly, keep in mind that David has an identity crisis when someone wants to give him something. Many of us are afraid to receive because we are so used to it being taken away or people walking away. The king wanted to reward him. He didn't mind fighting battles for the king; he just minded receiving from the king. Being Christ-confident is about opening ourselves up to receive. We can't be saved without receiving.

> *"Then Peter said unto them, Repent and be baptized every one of you in the name of Jesus Christ for the remission of sins, and ye shall receive the gift of the Holy Ghost"* (Acts 2:38).

David called his family nothing. Many of us are bitter, angry, insecure, and wounded over the projections of insecurities from our families. This is why parents must deal with their insecurities so that they won't be subconsciously suppressed and acted out on their children.

However, I have good news because it isn't healthy to continue blaming the family for our inadequate feelings. Your insecurities might have come from your family. Still, your confidence must come from the Lord Jesus Christ, our God and Savior.

What is Low Self-esteem?

As a mental health counselor in the field, one of the biggest challenges is getting my clients to admit that they battle with low self-esteem. One of my friends said, "when I hear 'low self-esteem,' I think it means a person is low." That is not the case at all. One can be rich and have low self-esteem. One can be beautiful and feel ugly. One can be at the top of their game, feeling like a failure simultaneously.

Low self-esteem is a thought pattern that stems from a belief that we are inadequate. Individuals can be highly capable, gifted, and reminded of their accomplishments. Regardless of how many affirmations we give, it isn't enough because they have sealed the deal of accepting those insecurities by believing them. If someone believes a lie, it's true to them. The devil knows that it is impossible to please God without faith (Hebrews 11:6). His best way to attack our faith in Christ is to affect our confidence.

> *So do not throw away this confident trust in the Lord. Remember the great reward it brings you (Hebrews 10:35, NLT).*

Many believers come to Christ, get baptized in his name and filled with the Holy Spirit, and still aren't walking in the joy of the Lord Jesus. They have changed their lives but haven't changed how they see themselves. The Bible teaches and encourages the saints of God to *"be renewed in the spirit of your mind" (Ephesians 4:23)*. It doesn't satisfy our soul to change our lives for Christ without changing our perception of ourselves in Christ.

David did not handle his success by becoming arrogant. He gave all glory to the highest God. David knew that *"If it had not been for the LORD who was on our side"* (*Psalms 124:1*).

Many with low self-esteem often overcompensate for insecurities. I want to encourage you are constantly overcompensating for deep-seated insecurities: you don't have to overdo it to do well. Do what God has called you to do with confidence and get some sleep.

Self-Esteem Vs. Christ-Esteem

Self-esteem is not always good at handling rejection. Some rejections can bring the strongest individual to their knees. Christ-confidence is all about knowing that we don't get to choose who we lose. We cannot control who stays. The Christ-confident individual knows that if someone walks out of their life regardless of how hard they have tried to show them consistency, love, and support, the will of God must be behind it.

Self-confidence is also reliant on self to gain knowledge or the knowledge of the wrong people. The Christ-confident individual knows that they can trust the word of God and the comfort of His Holy Spirit for guidance. God's word and the Holy Ghost will never lie to the true believer. Many individuals have rejected God's call on their life because someone has rejected them. I will never forget a dear friend of mine who had gone out of his way to love a woman who was highly unappreciative and ungrateful. Everyone saw it but him. His co-workers tried to tell him, close friends tried to tell him, but he did not appear to accept it. One day, after they broke up, he said, "I turned my back on God for her." I want to encourage you to hold on tight to your purpose even if others think it's corny.

3. The Fear of Losing Control

A careful analysis of the Life of David shows us that David battled with a lot of anxiety. David feared for his life and worried about things going wrong. David even had moments of paranoia. Let's first look at his anxiety and then paranoia.

> *[10] So David escaped from Saul and went to King Achish of Gath. [11] But the officers of Achish were unhappy about his being there. "Isn't this David, the king of the land?" they asked. "Isn't he the one the people honor with dances, singing, 'Saul has killed his thousands, and David his ten thousand'?" [12] David heard these comments and was very afraid of what King Achish of Gath might do to him. [13] So he pretended to be insane, scratching on doors and drooling down his beard. (1 Samuel 21:10-13, NLT).*

David was gifted, anointed, and intelligent. He was a man of war and a powerful musician. What made him act insane? Fear is the answer. It happens to the best of us. David, who is known in the Bible for singing, dancing before the LORD with all his might, and writing psalms of trust in the LORD his God, is now acting insane. Let's go back for a moment to the singing of the ten thousand David killed:

> *[5] Whatever Saul asked David to do, David did it successfully. So Saul made him a com-*

mander over the men of war, an appoint-
ment welcomed by the people and Saul's
officers alike.[6] When the victorious Israelite
army was returning home after David had
killed the Philistine, women from all the
towns of Israel came out to meet King Saul.
They sang and danced for joy with tambou-
rines and cymbals.[a] 7 This was their song:
"Saul has killed his thousands, and David
his ten thousand!" 8 This made Saul very
angry. "What's this?" he said. "They credit
David with ten thousand and me with only
thousands. Next, they'll be making him
their king!" 9 So, from that time on, Saul
kept a jealous eye on David. (1 Samuel
18:5-9, NLT).

David is drooling on his beard and purposely acting insane out of fear and anxiety. Catch this. His fear and anxiety are due to what made him successful. In 1 Samuel 21, he's afraid of the same thing he was celebrated for in 1 Samuel 18. King Saul had sent him out to battle.

The battle was a success, but the song the women of Jerusalem sang made Saul envy the young soon to be king. *Saul has killed his thousands, and David his ten thousand! (1 Samuel 18:7).*

The king could not be fully happy for David because he envied the young boy. Many don't hate you; they just can't resist the temptation to envy you. Nobody wakes up saying, "I want to be jealous today." Saul's jealousy caused him to fear David. What amazes me is that the Bible makes it clear he hates David simply because the LORD was with him (1 Samuel 18:12, NLT). David used to relax and enjoy that song. Now he gets afraid and nervous when he hears it because he's on the run.

Many of us are afraid to enjoy the celebratory moments in our lives because we fear it is the calm before the storm. David was not used to a celebration as he was often criticized. That he knew how to deal with, he trusted God with his enemies. However, trusting God with the celebration was new to David. In his embryonic stages of naivete, he thought that everyone loved him at the celebratory moment of his life. Many of us have been betrayed at our celebrations by people we have invited to join the successful moments of our lives that Christ afforded us, that we are afraid to celebrate again.

David knew that God prepared a table for him in the presence of his enemies. Still, David had to learn to stay seated when backstabbers had a reserved seat at the party. David was drooling on his beard, acting out of control because he was afraid to lose control. This is anxiety at its best. Many who are gifted, anointed, and called by God don't know how to enjoy the success that the Lord Jesus has granted. It's hard to enjoy something you're expecting to end.

When our confidence has been shaken to the core from the many losses in our lives, whether it's a loss of a relationship, esteem, opportunities, or positions, we become procrastinators at maximizing the moment. Instead of focusing on going higher, we worry about how low we can go. Major losses will take a toll on our emotional wellbeing to the degree to which we choose safety over risks.

This Even Plays Out in Relationships

Dana was shocked that Nick took an interest in her. He was a college football star, and she was a rape victim. That's what she called herself. As his game schedule increased, they were not spending as much time together as they did initially. When Nick was busy with games and practices, she would call out of work on days she knew he would call her. She also canceled her plans to go to her book club meetings, basically giving up her life when she wasn't with him.

Then they got married. She thought that they would spend every waking moment together. Nick would make more time for his wife, but she became more anxious when he was away from the phone. She secretly vowed to show him she could be the perfect wife, not realizing that she had already won him over, which was why he proposed to her in the first place.

Nick did his best to affirm his wife as much as he could. He would FaceTime her, send her flowers, and plan surprise visits for her in the evenings. It just wasn't enough. He encouraged her to go back to the book club and find things she enjoyed. Dana only interpreted that as Nick not wanting to be around her. Out of despair and insecurity, she tried to control him, which failed (because we can't control others to alleviate our insecurities).

Nick grew tired after five years and asked for a divorce. Dana's heart dropped as her biggest fears were put into words. Overwhelmed by anxiety, she fell into a depression. She had made her husband her life by giving up her life. Her mind went straight back to when she was raped. She told herself, "I guess I'm only good for screwing and leaving."

Self-Confidence vs. Christ-Confidence

Dana's insecurities caused her to behave in ways that made her lose the very thing that she made her life: her husband. Self-confidence places its hope in people, places, and things, in the name of self. Christ-Confidence says, "Some nations boast of their chariots and horses, but we boast in the NAME of the LORD our God" (Psalms 20:7, NLT). Dana didn't realize that the Bible made it clear that "Christ, who is our life…" (Colossians 3:4, NLT) is the only one we give up our lives for.

Self-confidence often causes us to think that we have attained what we have because of accomplishments, sweat, and hard work. The only problem with that is we can become so focused on what we think we accomplish to the degree to which we think we have to control it. Christ- confidence is all about knowing that I cannot control who comes or stays. Christ-confident individuals know that because of the purpose and call of Christ in their lives, everyone who comes will not stay. Christ's confidence is all about knowing that if I lose someone, it must be accepted as the will of God and not a character defect. When we have experienced an ample amount of rejection, neglect, or abandonment, we often lower our expectations to prevent experiencing any further pain because we don't expect others to stay anyway. Christ-confidence is all about learning to see loss through the eyes of faith in Christ. Don't lower your expectations because you've lost a few people. **Remember, low expectations will feed low self-esteem.**

Remember, low expectations will feed low self-esteem.

You Do You, and I'll Do Me

The word of God tells the body of Christ to be doers of the word and not hearers only (James 1:22). What is the consequence of reading the Bible without applying it? Deception. "But be ye doers of the word, and not hearers only, *deceiving yourselves*" (James 1:22).

Notice the word selves. **Once again, Jesus Christ never taught self-esteem; Christ taught Christ-confidence. To obey the word is how we grow in Christ-confidence.** However, many of us feel like we are too hurt, weak, wounded, and too tired to obey the word right now. Instead of doing the word, we just "do me." This is an urban expression for "I do what I want to do." This may manifest itself in becoming an over-achiever, a manifestation of inferiority. We feel like we have to prove to the world

Once again, Jesus Christ never taught self-esteem; Christ taught Christ-confidence. To obey the word is how we grow in Christ-confidence.

how good, great, and gifted we are to feel better about ourselves. Then, when we feel like we have not received the recognition we deserved, we become anxious or depressed.

Others become underachievers. Out of fear and anxiety (which are the twin supports of low self-esteem), some don't take risks for fear of failing. It's not that they are not capable, talented, or gifted. Some have the resources, time, and money but don't have the courage. Let's be clear: You don't have to be confident to be courageous. However, if we walk in Christ-confidence, being courageous will just flow.

4. The Fear of the Past Showing Up Again

Some flirt with their past. Others hang out with their past. Some sleep around with their past. Nevertheless, some of us can't afford to return to what the Lord Jesus delivered us from. Going back to an old lover, a profession that God told you to leave, the people Christ told us to leave, or places we used to hide out and sin at. Some try to avoid the temptation of going back, but David thought he had to go back.

> *8 David asked Ahimelech, "Do you have a spear or sword? The king's business was so urgent that I didn't even have time to grab a weapon!" 9 "I only have the sword of Goliath the Philistine, whom you killed in the valley of Elah," the priest replied. "It is wrapped in a cloth behind the ephod. Take that if you want it, for there is nothing else here." There is nothing like it!" David replied. "Give it to me!"10 So David escaped from Saul and went to King Achish of Gath" (1 Samuel 21:8-10)*

You remember when David fought Goliath, right? Saul was afraid to go after the nine-foot-tall giant but not David. When David came out to fight Goliath, He laughed at David. David reminded him, "You come to me with a sword, spear, and javelin, but I come to you in the name of the LORD of Heaven's Armies – the God of the armies of Israel, whom you defied" (1 Samuel 17:45, NLT). David's confidence wasn't in the sword of Goliath back then; his confidence was in the name of the LORD. He even reminded us that "Our help is in the name of the Lord, who made heaven and earth" (Psalms 124:8).

It was the name of the Lord Jesus that brought victory over Goliath. The sword is just an instrument that David used. The sword was the resource, but the name of the LORD was his source. This is why we make a big deal out of the name of

Jesus Christ, for He is the LORD of all. You may be saying, "I don't see the name Jesus in the Old Testament." Jehovah was the name that God was called. Jesus, in the New Testament, means "Jehovah is salvation." The last time I checked, there was only one Jehovah. There is only one God who bears the name Jehovah. If Jesus means, "Jehovah is salvation," that can only mean one thing: Jesus is God (Colossians 2:9).

David is not as confident in 1 Samuel 21 as in 1 Samuel 17. He is looking for the sword of Goliath when he should have been relying on the name of the LORD. Many of us don't want to face another betrayal, so we avoid making new friends. We rationalize our fears by saying to ourselves, "I keep my circle small." We don't want to fail academically anymore, so we choose a convenient major for our anxieties and insecurities. We want to get married, but we won't pick someone who is too attractive because we think someone that good-looking can't be faithful to us.

Embarrassment is Normal

It's not so much the incident as the feelings that give us anxiety. One of the reasons why many of us don't want to go through the same pain again is because we don't want to feel the humiliation of anxiety, depression, devastation, and despair.

Janelle had gone through many failed relationships, where every man cheated on her. By the time she met Tray, she was already skeptical of him because his name was connected to a negative connotation of "black men who cheat." However, the other guys who cheated on her were Richard, James, Clarence, and Todd. It was Todd who shook her emotions to her core.

After coming home from working a double shift at a hospital, Janelle decided to make Todd a candlelight dinner. She waited up for him until one in the morning. There were no responses, no texts, and no check-ins. She felt stupid, and a sense of anxiety came over her. Sadly, she makes one final phone call before bed. He called back, but his phone went to voicemail after waking up to the ringtone at three in the morning.

The phone rings again, and he accidentally calls her back as some phones do. She answers but instantly hears the lovemaking sounds in the background. She vows to herself to never trust him again. Then came Tray. He was nothing but a gentleman to her. However, this was the first time at night that he had not answered her call. She experienced a familiar emotional roller coaster as she recalls the night she overheard Todd cheating on her with another woman on the phone. Though Tray would never put her in that situation, she is still traumatized by her last relationship that something like a simple missed call could set her spiraling.

Insecurity will make us uncomfortable around innocent people. Fearing a fear that does not exist (Psalms 53:5). Janelle was embarrassed before by Todd and was not about to look stupid with what she feared Tray might do. Ultimately, the weight of her insecurities was too much for her.

Janelle could not be convinced that Tray would not cheat on her as Todd did. It is true that "what we fear, we create." After losing all he had, Job made the statement: "What I always feared has happened to me" (Job 3:25, NLT).

Self-Confidence vs. Christ-Confidence

Self-confident individuals know that everyone has an embarrassing moment. They are not going to let a few embarrassments stop them. However, Christ-confident individuals are aware that any embarrassing moment in their life does not happen by accident. They may hurt, but that hurt is not based on insecurities. That hurt is predicated on the humanity of the believer. Christ-confident individuals know that God allowed it for his purpose and his glory.

Self-confident individuals want to protect what they have because they worked hard for it and know they have earned it. Neither do self-confident individuals live in fear of losing someone.

They have learned to accept it, heal, and move on. However, Christ-confident individuals know that we will lose some people because of who we are in Christ. This does not mean we are not valuable. It's because of our value that some people have to go. We have learned to accept it as God's will and keep praising him.

Getting Through vs. Going Along

Fear and anxiety have the power to control one's life if we allow it. The Bible called fear a spirit. *For God has not given us a spirit of fear and timidity, but of power, love, and self-discipline (2 Timothy 1:7, NLT).* In my clinical work as a counselor, we are trained to look at the functional impairments of a client's diagnosis, such as occupational, environmental, family, and social impairments. In other words, is the client's depression affecting their work or school production, decreasing the harmony in the home, and overall affecting their quality of life.

Remember, fear and anxiety cannot do severe damage without feelings of inferiority. The devil cannot harass the believer's mind until he can get us to feel insecure about ourselves. The enemy will know he got through to you and won your confidence over him when your insecurities affected your purpose and calling. Have you given up on your passions because you think you won't thrive out of anywhere? Have you been procrastinating so long that you don't see the point in getting started now? Maybe you've allowed others whose opinion you valued to talk you out of what Christ has called you to do.

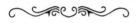

If you have to backslide to stay with somebody, they are the wrong somebody for you.

Some are so paralyzed by unhealthy self-worth that they go along to get along. One of my friends used to say, "Curtis, I lie about eating his food just to avoid confrontation." Sidebar: **if you have to backslide to stay with somebody, they are the wrong somebody for you.** Hear me good: As long as you go along to get along, you won't get to see what you could be. You owe it to yourself to become your best.

"Come On Over to My Place"

Others don't go along to get along. They're on the go. They refuse to be passive. They are determined to be the best possible version of themselves. The only problem is they are running to the beat of someone else's drum. I will never forget the story of a guy I will call Raymond Oxford. Raymond was a big stockbroker with a wife and six children. He had the kind of life most men would envy. However, while we were devastated by the events of September 11, 2001, his wife was still traumatized by September 10, 2001.

That was the day her husband drove to a hotel room by himself and shot himself in the head. She was shocked that her husband, who appeared to be so sure of himself, dependable, self-reliant, would take his own life. She later stated that she realized that he never ran to the beat of his drum. He never lived the life he wanted, but one that others chose for him. She said that those were reasons he completed suicide.

Many of you may remember the song by Teddy Pendergrass, *Come On Over to My Place*. It speaks about his desire to get his woman to his place, where it was quiet. Well, the space that Raymond occupied in that lonely hotel room was not the place someone called him over to. His voice drove him there. Please don't be defeated by your voice. I will deal with your voice in a later chapter. As for now, I will leave you with the words of Dr. Freddy Haynes, "When you dance to someone else's rhythm, they will leave you singing the blues."

PART 2

Misdiagnosed

THREE

When Self-Esteem Attacks

*Don't think you are better than you are.
Be honest in your evaluation of yourselves,
measuring yourselves by the faith God has
given us—Romans 12:3, NLT*

"*P*erfect Patty messed up! Perfect Patty messed up!" These were the words of a wife who tried to play the everything-is-perfect role, costing her mental health. In the movie, *Why Did I Get Married?* Janet Jackson plays the role of Patricia, who is married to Gavin, played by Malik Yoba. They are both successful middle-class African Americans who have done well for themselves. Patricia is a psychologist and college professor, narrating her book, "*Why Did I Get Married?*" to her students.

She is also a voice of reason to her circle of friends in the movie, who occasionally get to hear her unsolicited advice. This movie is about four married couples asking, "why did I get married?" to one another. The road trip should not be too much of a question to ponder because they have a psychologist in their midst: Dr. Patricia, aka "Perfect Patty." While Perfect Patty is trying to assist her friends in exploring the core conflict of their marital problems, she is suppressing some guilt from a trauma in her marriage with Gavin.

Perfect Patty accidentally left their son in the car seat unstrapped. Gavin was upset with her for a while but never verbalized it. He only told his boys. While on the trip, the couples have a few drinks, and an intoxicated person "tells no tales." So, Mike reveals to Patricia that Gavin came crying to him at the table, not understanding how Patricia can be so stupid to leave the baby unstrapped in the car. Perfect Patty looks at him with anger and hurt written all over her face.

Subsequently, there is silent tension in the air when they return home that can only be addressed through love, understanding, and humility. When Gavin attempts to show Patricia the picture of their deceased son, she doesn't want to look. She loses her cool and blurts out, "Perfect, Patty messed up! Perfect Patty messed up." She prided herself on being the perfect mother, wife, friend, professor, and psychologist that she couldn't properly grieve the death of her son. It wasn't just the guilt of knowing she did not strap him safely in his car seat, but it was also the pain of having to admit to herself that she wasn't as perfect as she portrayed herself to be. In essence, what happened to Patricia when her husband tried to get her to face the music about the son's death, her avoidance was a self-esteem attack.

Do Psychiatrists Know Where Anxiety Attacks Come From?

Anyone who knows me knows I love to study human behavior. When treating a client who presents with stress, depression, and anxiety symptoms, it is pivotal that mental health professionals treat the core conflict of the client's problem. In my research and study on the mind related to the field of counseling, it has been proven that most psychiatrists are not diagnosing the real problem. Dr. William Glasser, a psychiatrist known for reality therapy, observed this phenomenon.

He stated in an interview, "Stay as far away from the DSM-5 as possible." Remember, the DSM-5 is the *Diagnostic and Statistical Manual of Mental Disorders (DSM)*. This is the book that most therapists, clinical/counseling psychologists, and clinical psychiatrists diagnose their clients. Also, keep in mind this book is also how most mental health professionals get paid through the billing codes in that DSM-5, connected to insurance.

Even though most mental health professionals are required by the American Counseling Association (ACA) and American Psychological Association (APA) code of ethics to use this book, not all therapists, clinical/counseling psychologists, and clinical psychiatrists agree. Dr. Allen Francis, M.D., who was on the committee that edited this book, made this statement:

"The publication of DSM-5 is a sad moment for psychiatry and a risky one for patients. My recommendation for clinicians is simple. Don't use the DSM-5" (Rosenthal, p. 536). In other words, he believed that a worldwide book would misdiagnose many patients.

Then, Dr. Sorensen spoke truth to power with her work on self-esteem. She informs us that depression and anxiety are not the core issue of an individual's problem. They are simply the symptom and not the root. Talk to any good psychologist that will be honest, and they will tell you that symptoms alone do not qualify a client to have a disorder. The client must have those symptoms for a certain duration. Those symptoms have caused functional impairments, affecting the individual's everyday life. For example, one cannot be diagnosed with clinical depression if sad sporadically. They must have met the criteria for depressed symptoms that last for more than two weeks, according to the DSM-5.

In addition to Avoidant Personality Disorder and Social Anxiety Disorder, the following diagnoses are also frequently and inappropriately given to people who suffer from low self-esteem. In nearly all cases, the problem presented to the therapist is the result of low self-esteem but can be misdiagnosed and therefore mistreated.

- Major depression and other depressive disorders
- Dependent Personality Disorder
- Eating disorders
- Borderline Personality Disorder

Seeing low self-esteem as a symptom of each of these is a significant mistake because low self-esteem should be the primary diagnosis. Eating disorders and most cases of depression and anxiety are the results of low self-esteem, not the other way around. Still, there is no diagnosis in the manual for low self-esteem. However, it is frequently listed as a symptom of another diagnosis. Low self-esteem is not considered a mental health problem but rather is labeled as either a psychosocial or psychoeducational issue; classifications are considered far less serious than those named in the diagnostic manual. *The absence of a category for low self-esteem amplifies the fact that low self-esteem is not taken seriously, nor is it widely understood, even by the most experienced and most widely respected people in the field of psychology (Sorensen, p. 91-92).*

You Have to Choose to Be Christ-Confident

I love what I do as a therapist; however, I'm a preacher who esteems the Bible above my own opinion. So, I'm not a therapist who happens to be a preacher. I'm a preacher who happens to be a therapist. So, in training, therapists are taught about various psychologists who paved the way for upcoming therapists, counselors, psychologists, and psychiatrists. We are taught about Sigmund Freud and his theory on the Oedipus complex, Erick Erickson and his eight stages of development, Abraham Maslow, and his hierarchy of needs. Just to name a few. However, the psychiatrist whose work was close to the Bible was Dr. William Glasser.

Dr. Glasser is known for his work in Reality Therapy, which he also developed what he called Choice Theory. This theory suggests that we cannot control another person's behavior.

We can only control our own. He accentuates that we have a choice over how to choose to respond to the atrocities of life. His theory was close to the Holy Scriptures. The Bible teaches us that we have a choice, even when it comes to God.

"Choose ye this day whom ye will serve" (Joshua 24:15).

"I call heaven and earth as witnesses today against you, that I have set before you, life and death, blessing and cursing; therefore, choose life, that both you and your descendants live" (Deuteronomy 30:19, NKJV). Just to name a few, psychologically speaking, our choices will either accelerate or decelerate our confidence. Many are secretly battling regret stemming from insecurities from past decisions because they did not know who they were.

I once heard someone say, "One of the mistakes we ask our kids is 'What do you want to be when you grow up?' Instead, we should ask our children, 'Who do you want to be when you grow up?'" I wanted to be a barber, attorney, history teacher, police officer, and much more when I was a kid. Before you choose an occupation, choose Jesus. Before you choose a career, choose Jesus. Then, once you choose Christ, choose yourself. Many of us are having trouble choosing ourselves because we have not chosen Christ first. When Christ is our confidence, insecurities cannot find a resting place in our minds.

If you're a control freak, you aren't a happy individual. I have never met a happy, controlling person. Never! And I am pretty sure that I will never find one either. One of the major consequences of being a real control freak is severe anxiety attacks. Often what most psychiatrists and psychologists call a panic attack or an anxiety attack is really what Sorensen calls a self-esteem attack. **A self-esteem attack occurs when we face a situation or experience an event that triggers the insecurities we secretly believe about ourselves.**

A self-esteem attack occurs when we face a situation or experience an event that triggers the insecurities we secretly believe about ourselves.

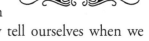

What makes a self-esteem attack powerful is what we secretly tell ourselves when we are in the thick of the event. Let me give you a scenario to exemplify what I mean:

> *Brad has a supportive, loving, and understanding wife, who loves Brad for who he is. Brad is happy to have her, but he is secretly amazed that she chose to marry someone like him. He does not think he is handsome at all. He thinks the real reason why his wife*

married him is that he is a nice guy who provides and would never cheat on her. As happy as he is with her, he feels a dark cloud come over him every time they go to the gym together. When he sees someone more physically fit than him come over to where they are working, he feels like he is choking, experiences racing thoughts, and has an increased heart rate. On the way home from the gym, he gives his wife, Shakirah, the silent treatment. They have been married for twelve years, so she is aware that her husband is acting jealous. What she is not mindful of is the fact that he had a self-esteem attack right in front of her at the gym.

Notice that Brad experienced all the symptoms of someone with a panic or anxiety attack.

Brad experienced choking, racing thoughts, and increased heart rate. Shakirah just thinks she has a jealous husband; she is unable to understand that he secretly has moderate self-esteem attacks. His primary physician simply refers to them as panic attacks. It's not Brad's desire to think, feel, and be a jealous husband. Brad knows he can be jealous at times but doesn't know how to stop it. **Many anxieties and panic attacks are low self-esteem driven.** Below is a list of incidents that can trigger self-esteem attacks:

Many anxieties and panic attacks are low self-esteem driven.

- Being rejected by someone you love
- Thinking you can never do anything right

- Misinterpreting a joke
- Not performing well
- Being stared at
- Feeling like everyone takes your kindness for weakness
- Hearing your spouse say they want a divorce
- Feeling disrespected
- Not having your phone call returned
- Not being appreciated
- Seeing your friends post pictures at an event on Facebook and didn't invite you
- Feeling like your opinions and ideas are being downplayed

Now what is listed above are just a few triggering incidents that can precipitate a self-esteem attack. Now the severity of the self-esteem attack is predicated on a few foundational factors:

- The level of attention given to them
- The support or lack thereof from the support systems
- The duration of focus – the longer focus is misinterpreted, the more challenging it appears to overcome
- Thought patterns and perceptions of the incident that is triggering – in other words, the more extreme view of the consequences of the situation that brought on the self-esteem attack
- The extent of progress in coping with self-esteem attacks

How Much Worse Can I Feel After A Self-Esteem Attack?

After a self-esteem attack, it is expected for one to feel sorry for themselves. You may beat yourself up for not being able to control your emotions, not understanding that emotions are not bad. It's our thinking that creates these negative emotions. Additionally, it is also possible to feel like it's the end of the world, as if there is no hope for you. Don't be surprised when Satan starts talking to you in your voice, calling you stupid, soft, or ugly. The devil wants to make sure you stay insecure forever. Too late, devil! You already have the book in your hand!

It is also expected to feel weak, crying for days. Sometimes you may wonder why you may have been given the short end of the stick in life. **It's not your fault; it's your perception.** Sometimes, based on the severity of one's low self-esteem, the

It's not your fault; it's your perception.

embarrassment may feel more humiliating than the self-esteem attack itself.

I'm Through Trying

After one or two good self-esteem attacks, many are tempted never to try again. We want to avoid feelings of anxiety, despair, embarrassment, and shame. This angers and frustrates our friends and loved ones, who see our potential and gifts. They see no reason for us to quit.

This is one of the key differences between anxiety and depression. Depression makes sense to others when we explain it. Anxiety is something that only we can see. Why is that? **Anxiety has a lot to do with how we see ourselves more than how we interpret the situation.**

Anxiety has a lot to do with how we see ourselves more than how we interpret the situation.

Stage Fright

Many of us are praying for moments that we are afraid to embrace. It's not because we don't want it. We have been visualizing it for so long; we have prayed about it for years, even rehearsed it when no one was around. The issue is that we don't think we can handle what we prayed for. We doubt we can maintain it after it's given to us. More importantly, we are consumed with how others will react if they don't like the gift, call, and anointing on our lives.

Many of us are highly gifted, anointed, and talented; nevertheless, our gifts do not have the desired impact on others that we wish because they are infiltrated with our fears and anxieties. I once heard someone say, "Don't do your best when you aren't at your best." However, how do you do your best when you think the worst of yourself? Low self-esteem doesn't stop us from being gifted. However, it can hinder us from displaying our gift at full capacity. When we are unsure of ourselves, we won't enjoy ourselves successfully.

"Don't Embarrass Me."

¹⁴ And David danced before the LORD with all his might, wearing a priestly garment. [a] ¹⁵ So David and all the people of Israel brought up the Ark of the LORD with shouts of joy and the blowing of rams' horns.[16] But as the Ark of the LORD entered the City of David, Michal, the daughter of Saul, looked down from her window. When she saw King David leaping and dancing before the LORD, she was contemptuous for him.[17] They brought the Ark of the LORD and set it in its place inside the special tent David had prepared for it. And David sacrificed burnt offerings and peace offerings to the LORD. [18] When he had finished his sacrifices, David blessed the people in the name of the LORD of Heaven's Armies. [19] Then, he gave every Israelite man and woman in the crowd a loaf of bread, a cake of dates,[b] and a cake of raisins. Then all the people returned to their homes.[20] When David returned home to bless his own family, Michal, the daughter of Saul, came out to meet him. She said in disgust, "How distinguished the king of Israel looked today, shamelessly exposing himself to the servant girls as any vulgar person might do! (2 Samuel 6:14-20, NLT)

There is a valid reason why David is rejoicing. David is bringing back the Ark of Covenant which is symbolic of the presence of God. The last man who touched the Ark was killed on the spot (see 2 Samuel 6). King David was excited that God did not kill him. By the way, David's life was spared because he carried the Ark of Covenant God's way. David praises God with all his might. God had no problem with David's praise, but his wife did.

Michal was embarrassed that the king would act like that. She doesn't want her husband worshiping God in public. She loves her husband. In fact, in the past, she kept her father, Saul, from killing David, on one occasion. She just thinks praise is for private, not for a king in public. She is the only one in David's life who is embarrassed by him. How do you handle the acceptance you get from complete strangers, but you are told you are an embarrassment to the ones who say they love you?

Many are battling unhealthy self-worth because people close to them perceive them as an embarrassment. There are adults in their fifties and even sixties who battle how they view themselves based on those in their household who were always ashamed of them. What hurts more is when you love the people who are embarrassed by you. Some have gone through this for so long that they now see themselves as an embarrassment. David was not about to go out like that.

> *²¹ David retorted to Michal, "I was dancing before the LORD, who chose me above your father and all his family! He appointed me as the leader of Israel, the people of the LORD, so I celebrate before the LORD. ²² Yes, and I am willing to look even more foolish than this, even to be humiliated in my own eyes! But those servant girls you mentioned will indeed think I am distinguished" (2 Samuel 6:21-22, NLT).*

Don't get me wrong; King David had a lot of insecurities, fears, and anxieties that had bothered him for years of his life. Still, in God, David placed his confidence. King David had a Christ-confidence about him that he wouldn't allow his wife to get in the way.

He put it this way: "My flesh and my heart may fail, But God is the strength of my heart and my portion forever" (Psalms 73:26, NASB).

The enemy will often talk through the people we love to keep us from walking in our divine purpose and calling in Christ Jesus. **Sometimes if you want to know what Christ is calling us into, just look out for what the people we love are trying to talk us out of.**

Sometimes if you want to know what Christ is calling us into, just look out for what the people we love are trying to talk us out of.

I Don't Want People to Think I'm Arrogant

Many of us grew up in families where we might not have received a lot of praise because our parents/caregivers did not want us to become too proud or arrogant. They wanted us to stay humble, not get beside ourselves. Consequently, that did not always do us too much good.

Many have become insecure, despite being gifted, because they have never been encouraged or told they were good enough. Then when God opens the door to put your gift out on a national platform, allow you to start your own business, or connect you to kings, many of us will downplay our gift, so others won't think they are arrogant.

Because we did not get much positive affirmation, we are still seeking it from the people who knew us before or the people we are meeting now. That is a very dangerous position to be in.

The Lord Jesus Christ, God Almighty, is the only one who truly knows how to affirm us more than anyone. Once again, David reminds us that, "It is better to trust in the LORD than to put confidence in man" (Psalms 118:8).

I want to encourage you that you aren't that little kid anymore that has to make sure you don't shine so bright, dimming your light, so others won't think you are too proud. Christ wants you to use what he gave you with confidence as long as it's Christ-confidence.

You Wouldn't Believe It if I Said It Anyway

What can make the heart race faster, trigger insecurities, and heighten our anxiety is when we think the compliments we get are just to make us feel better. Many of us have believed that we were incompetent for so long that we question and accuse others of patronizing us that tell us otherwise. Begin to pray, asking the Lord Jesus to show you who you can trust and who you can't. King David had been betrayed so much that he wrote, "In my anxiety, I cried out to you, "These people are all liars" (Psalms 116:11, NLT). Everyone in David's life was not a liar; only the people who lied to him were liars.

I Don't Remember

There is an old saying where I come from that says, "Everybody that plays crazy is not crazy."

That statement carries an impossible truth to it. However, some people cursed us out, called us out by name, and told us we wouldn't be anything. Then guess what? Once we confronted them, they said, "Oh, I don't remember that." Many with anger issues forget what they said when they lashed out like a drunk man doesn't remember what he said.

Why is that? Studies have revealed that memory loss manifests the after-effects of a self-esteem attack.

Sorensen states,

> "When the person with low self-esteem is in the throes of a self-esteem attack, his anxiety may be so great that he experiences periods of memory loss. He may be so upset that he does not hear what is being said and may have no memory afterward of what he just said. He may not remember an entire conversation or incident at a later time. Usually, within a few minutes, the anxiety has subsided. He will be calmer and more mindful of what is happening around him. However, he may never recall what occurred during those few seconds of extreme anxiety" (Sorensen, pg. 88).

One of the primary reasons many with self-esteem attacks suffer memory loss is because they spent so much time becoming a master expert at putting those moments out of their minds. They use forgetting the incident as a defense mechanism to cope with the incident. Like Dr. Jamal Bryant put it, real peace is "having the memory without the pain attached to it."

The good news about being filled with the Spirit of Christ (the Holy Spirit) is that He will bring all the right things back to a memory for the building up of our Christ-confidence (John 14:26).

Christ will not harass your mind with thoughts of insecurity, self-doubt, and anxiety. The Bible says, "And now, dear brothers and sisters, one final thing. Fix your thoughts on what is true, honorable, right, pure, and lovely, and admirable. Think about things that are excellent and worthy of praise" (Philippians 4:8, NLT).

Self-Confidence vs. Christ-Confidence

Many with unhealthy self-esteem suffer from self-esteem attacks that naturally confident individuals cannot relate to. If you battle insecurities, don't get discouraged. Many people understand where you are coming from. Now let's not get these twisted self-confident individuals to have devastating moments where they are upset, angry, devastated, and overwhelmed. The difference is in their reactions. Self-confident individuals don't react; they respond.

They know it is not over because they experienced a crisis, traumatic event, or some bouts of dysfunction. Now the Christ-confident individual has human moments, where they get heartbroken, discouraged, and lonely. However, after they feel the feelings and process their thoughts, they remind themselves of who they are in Christ Jesus the Lord God. Here is an example of Christ-confidence when you're overwhelmed:

> *"Three days later, when David and his men arrived home at their town of Ziklag, they found that the Amalekites had made a raid into the Negev and Ziklag; they had crushed Ziklag and burned it to the ground. ² They had carried off the women and children and everyone else but without killing anyone.³ When David and his*

men saw the ruins and realized what had happened to their families, ⁴ they wept until they could weep no more. ⁵ David's two wives, Ahinoam from Jezreel and Abigail, the widow of Nabal from Carmel, were among those captured. ⁶ David was now in great danger because all his men were very bitter about losing their sons and daughters, and they began to talk of stoning him. But David found strength in the LORD his God" (1 Samuel 30:1-6, NLT).

1. Incident: David's hometown is burned with fire, and wives and children are taken captive.
2. Self-esteem attack: David is overwhelmed because his men talked about killing him. David allowed himself to cry until there were no more tears in life.
3. Christ-confident: David found strength in God.

Think about some moments in your life where you would have completely lost your mind in the middle of a crisis, and when others who cried with you have now turned on you if you did not have a relationship with the Lord Jesus Christ. If you are not saved and are tired of going through a crisis and betrayal alone, let me offer you the plan of salvation: "Repent and be baptized every one of you in the name of Jesus Christ for the remission of sins, and ye shall receive the gift of the Holy Ghost" (Acts 2:38).

Responding to the Self-Esteem Attack

Remember that the root of most panic and anxiety attacks is self-esteem attacks. Different terminology but the same thoughts, feelings, and behavior. What makes these self-esteem attacks dreadful is that we do not know how to respond to them. Here are some tools on how to respond to the next triggering incidents and stop them before they overwhelm you:

1. Think back to the last time you experienced a self-esteem attack. Ask yourself what you thought about yourself at that moment. For example, the last self-esteem attack might have occurred when you walked in on your spouse cheating. Did you feel betrayed? Of course! Were you hurt? Absolutely! Did you want revenge? Probably. The real question is, what did you think about yourself? Did you think there was something wrong with you that caused him to cheat?

2. Ask yourself why do you believe in what you believe about yourself? Do you believe that you were cheated on because, deep down, you already decided no matter what, no one would be faithful to you? We will not live any better than we choose to believe. The self-esteem attack triggered events and circumstances of what we believe about ourselves.

3. Examine your behaviors when you feel this way. Do you go off on people when they secretly make you feel inferior? Do you lash out at the people you love in the middle of a self-esteem attack? Do you get a drink to calm your nerves?

4. Change your internal dialogue (Chapter 6 will cover this in-depth). We can indeed talk ourselves into a nervous breakdown. We become convinced by the things that we tell ourselves. Many individuals have calmed their fears and soothe their anxieties by talking themselves through and out of them. Next time you feel a sense of rejection, for instance, tell yourself that you are still valuable, even if the ones you wanted to accept you do not agree.

Don't Let Fear and Anxiety Stop You from Doing it Again.

I get it. Sometimes we have been hurt so long, devastated so much, and betrayed on a level we don't have the words to explain to the degree which we don't want to dust ourselves off, get on our feet, and go after what Christ put in our heart and in our spirit. Let me tell you that regret is a debilitating thing that will have us singing our "should have, could have, would have been" later down the road. Even when we go after what Christ has in store for us, others may still not support us, bad days will come, some things will go wrong, and everyone won't accept us. That does not mean God does not value us. However, it does mean that we have to know how to encourage ourselves in the Lord Jesus, our God. The LORD told me to tell you this:

> *² When you go through deep waters, I will be with you. When you go through rivers of difficulty, you will not drown. You will not be burned up when you walk through the fire of oppression; the flames will not con-*

sume you.[3] For I am the LORD, *your God, the Holy One of Israel, your Savior. I gave Egypt as a ransom for your freedom; I gave Ethiopia[a] and Seba in your place. (Isaiah 43:2-3, NLT).*

FOUR

Acting Hurt

> "Always settling—thinking I'm not worth it."
> —Leandria Johnson

*Y*ou know exactly what I'm talking about. Don't front. Yes, you! I'm talking to you directly. I'm talking to you that procrastinates (which is the arrogant assumption that God will give you enough time later to do what He told you to do today). I'm talking to you who gets upset when others stand up to you and tell you what your enablers won't: No. I'm talking to you who says you never had a good man but turn down the good ones because they are boring. I'm talking about self-sabotage.

Sorensen describes self-sabotage as a "self-defeating behavior as anything we say or do or anything we fail to say or do, that is not our own best interest, or that defeats our purpose" (Sorensen, pg. 99). Self-sabotage is about not moving to action on our God-given call, utilizing the gifts Christ gave us for His glory and purpose, and enduring even when it appears to be too much to handle. Let's look at a few everyday life examples.

Scenario #1 – Bad Boy Loving Sandra

Sandra constantly drains her girlfriends daily, frustrated with not having a good man. She is sick of the bad boys who treat her like dirt but wonders why she keeps attracting them. She does not understand that it's not her identity that attracts them; it's her thoughts about herself that do. Sandra has a male friend in her life that is very good to her and has expressed his love for her, demonstrated loyalty, and given her no reason to doubt his sincerity. However, she keeps him in the friend zone but constantly shows jealousy when other women show interest in him.

Scenario #2 – Opportunity Denying Orlando

Orlando has a talent for computers that do not compare. He has been working on computers since he was fifteen. He has fixed multiple computers for his family, friends, and even his company's CEO, where he is employed. However, he changes the subject when the opportunity to be the owner of his own company presents itself. He then talks about how much he likes his current job.

Scenario #3 – Desperate Bridesmaid Evette

She is tired of being the bridesmaid and never the bride. She congratulates her family members and friends on their weddings but secretly wonders when her turn will be. Her friends do not realize when she cries at weddings; it is not just for the happiness she feels for them. It is also for the sadness of only ever being a bridesmaid, going on forty-one.

Scenario #4 – Disobeying Preacher Jerry

Jerry has visions of messages he has been preaching. He states God has woken him out of his sleep. His Sunday school teacher gave him a call on his life for ministry. Jerry has even gotten physically ill for not obeying the command from God to preach. However, Jerry refuses to obey God because his dream is to be a full-time singer.

These are just a few of the many ways in which we self-sabotage emotionally, mentally, and spiritually. We want things that we don't take care of once we receive them. We pray for better but continue to chase worse. We feel constant disrespect but refuse to set boundaries. Self-sabotage is the unnecessary pain of not loving ourselves correctly.

Are We Waiting on Them or the Lord Jesus?

One degree of self-sabotage is rooted in stubbornness. When we are hurt, and that hurt sits for a long time, we may become stubborn. Sometimes, we act like we don't want the things we want in life so that we won't get hurt again. More importantly, we lower our expectations when we believe we are insignificant. One of the ways that we do that is by settling for the wrong people to turn into the right people.

The phenomenal poet and author herself, Maya Angelou, is known for her famous statement: "When someone shows you who they are, believe them." Many of us could have avoided the heartache if we had listened to those words from Ms. Angelou. This is what Jamar regretted as well.

Jamar was a preacher's son, raised in a Christian home, and had a father who taught him how to respect and treat a lady. He is also an established attorney for a thriving law firm. His family respects him, and his church loves him. The only problem is that his love life isn't where he wants it to be. Jamar seems to have difficulty finding a woman that won't take him for granted. It may not seem obvious that Jamar has been in several psychiatric hospitals for multiple suicide attempts. Yes, he is successful, makes over $85,000 a year, serves on the deacons board, and is acknowledged by the mayor of his city. However, that does not change that success does not compensate for **unhealthy self-esteem.**

Our culture is conditioned to believe that if we fix the externals, we will feel better on the inside. Men, who battle with insecurities, may think tinted windows and fancy rims will make them feel better about themselves. Some women feel that they can feel better about that breakup by getting their nails done or changing their hair. Even children who battle low self-esteem may fight other kids in school to feel better about themselves.

Jamar has a lot going for him. Nevertheless, he has been cheated on by the same woman multiple times, being physically abused by another, and emotionally abused by his daughter's mother. Sidebar: before you bring up the argument that the deacon, who was brought up in the church, has a baby out of wedlock, I want you to understand that where there is an intensity of insecurity, there will be a plethora of sin. Low self-esteem and unbelief are often the bedrock of continual backsliding. **We often sin or backslide to feel better about ourselves.**

We often sin or backslide to feel better about ourselves.

Jamar met a classy woman, Monica, at an event for his firm. She was a college professor and attorney herself. She was a published author with no children and never married. They were both the same age, and she believed in Jesus Christ. He talked to her for two months and became a couple for five months. He broke up with her by the sixth month to return to his ex, who physically abused him. Why? He thinks his love can change her. **It's hard to heal someone with the love we think we have for them when we don't know how to love ourselves.**

It's hard to heal someone with the love we think we have for them when we don't know how to love ourselves.

Let me explain what's happening with Jamar (that may be going on with you or someone you know). Jamar has never had a good relationship – Jamar's exes have cheated, physically abused

him, or mistreated him in some way. However, his exes are not the only ones to blame here. Jamar did not have the confidence to stand up for himself. Jamar did not have the Christ-confidence that we all desperately need. By the time he met Monica, he had liked her but didn't know how to receive genuine love from the woman because he felt it was too good to be true.

He sought counsel from his pastor, who suggested that he wait for his confidence to set in and get comfortable with Monica. Nevertheless, Jamar did not listen. He could not wait (one of the behavioral symptoms of low self-esteem is impulsivity) for God to help him get comfortable with the right one. Consequently, he sabotages the moment and women in his life, and he goes back to the same insecurities that may make him feel at home with himself.

Impulsive Insecurities

One of the most self-defeating behaviors we can ever perform is picking the wrong people for the right reason. **I always**

say don't settle for anyone when you feel like nobody just to be able to say you have somebody. Loneliness is no joke. If you don't believe it, think about the sad ending of comedian and actor Robin Williams. He was a great actor, made everyone laugh, and was the life of the party. Who knew the severity of his deep dark depression was tucked so well under his smile that it cost him his life?

I always say don't settle for anyone when you feel like nobody just to be able to say you have somebody.

August 11, 2014, was the day news reporters sent shock waves through the globe that the man who made everyone laugh died with Lewy Body Dementia. Notice that he died with a health condition; it's not the cause of death. Williams died from suicide. Additionally, he states, "I used to think the worst thing in life was to end up alone. It's not. The worst thing in life is to end up with people who make you feel alone." I think he spoke for so many individuals with that one statement.

If I am going to feel lonely, it will be based on having no one around. However, I refuse to be lonely around the people I let in my circle and my life. Many of us have grown tired of waiting on the Lord Jesus to send the right people in our lives to the degree to which we are tolerating anyone's company. People who love us have brought concerns to our attention that the person in our life is not good for us – so why do we continue to keep them around? The real reason is not that you don't want to be alone; it's because we have defined ourselves by some people or certain individuals who have made it clear verbally and through actions (or the lack thereof) that they only want to use us.

Let's face it; even a dog knows when they are loved or not. If you're doing all the calling, doing all the check-ins, and all the gas-wasting, you are chasing people who only want you at their convenience. That's a tough pill to swallow. Not loving who you are in Jesus Christ is even a tougher pill. Many of us are self-sabotaging who Christ will send into our lives because we are preoccupied with toxic people who are currently in our lives.

Self-Confidence vs. Christ-Confidence

Self-confident individuals get lonely, just like those who wrestle with insecurities. Self-confident people get tired of waiting for Mr. Right or Mrs. Right, just like those with low self-esteem. Self-confident individuals, however, don't allow a desperate moment, the need to be accepted, or living alone to make them make decisions out of their flesh. They know who they are. They know they are worth the wait. They might have made this mistake in the past, but they have forgiven themselves, refusing to go down that road of regret again. They also refuse to place themselves in that kind of predicament again.

On the other hand, a Christ-confident individual has a Christ perspective on waiting while alone. To be Christ-confident is to look at yourself and view your situation from God's perspective. A Christ-confident individual is aware that their loneliness is because of God's purpose. They know being alone is not an attack on their identity but a confirmation of their identity.

Areas That We Sabotage

1. Setting Boundaries

Many of us criticize ourselves when no one is around because we are angry with ourselves for not speaking up when we felt like we should have. We have allowed people to get away with murder because we felt so lucky to have them that we did not want to do anything to upset them and drive them away. When others have brought it to our attention that the individual was not right for us, we cursed them out, stopped speaking to them, or told them that they were jealous. However, secretly there was a gut feeling that your family and friends were right.

Suppose you're the type of individual that does not like to hurt others' feelings. In that case, chances are you will often find yourself surrounded by angry, authoritarian, or narcissistic people. They read you a mile away and are quite aware you have a problem with saying no. **The real issue is not them being around us; it's us not realizing who is within us.** "But you belong to God, my dear children. You have already won a victory over those people because the Spirit who lives in you is greater than the spirit who lives in the world" (1 John 4:4, NLT).

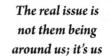

The real issue is not them being around us; it's us not realizing who is within us.

Many of us don't set boundaries because we are afraid to lose people. We don't want to say or do anything to set them off, so we suffer in silence. Anytime you have to give yourself up to be loved by someone else, a reevaluation must occur. If someone is trying to change everything about you, do they really like you? Think for a minute. There is a difference between character flaws and someone trying to dim your light. Venny made this same mistake.

Venny wrestled with low self-esteem all his life. Girls never gave him the time of day in middle or high school. He battled with suicidal ideations. He excelled in school and had a good job. His parents kept asking him when they were going to get grandchildren. They don't know that Venny's low self-esteem stems from the fact that he overheard his mom tell one of her sisters that she wished she had not had him during college because she wanted to get her degree first. Sadly, Venny only heard, "I wish I did not have him when I was in college."

The problem with Venny is that he doesn't trust his mother's words of affirmation after overhearing her say that when he was nine. Then he met Josephine. She was very toxic to Venny. She embarrassed him in public, talked down to him, and told him that she was only with him because she could not get back with her ex. Venny stayed with her because he felt lucky to have her. I know: you want to slap some sense into Venny, right? However, you're letting guilt, criticism, life, rumors, and your past treat you in any kind of way. When thoughts of guilt, fear, shame, and remorse harass us, what do we say back?

2. Finishing What You Started

A few years after my grandmother passed, I wanted to stop preaching. I didn't want to stop being saved. I just wanted to be a Christian without responsibility. I did not want to preach anymore. Life can hit you so hard to the degree we think there is no need to finish what we started. Many of us have dreams, goals, and a calling that Christ placed inside us that we have allowed others to talk us out of. Or maybe you've allowed your guilt to talk you out of it. You dropped out of school because you got depressed. Gave up on your marriage because someone else stood you up.

Or maybe you've compared your dream to someone else's and decided your dream is too small. You may be thinking your dream looks nothing like anyone else's. It's not supposed to look or mimic anyone else's. Christ gave it to you because he knows he equipped you for what he put inside of you. It gets frustrating and confusing when others don't understand or can't relate to what Christ has put inside of you. However, deep-seated self-doubt is at the core of your frustration that Christ did not give you. God didn't even give you the spirit of fear but of love, of power, and of a sound mind (2 Timothy 1:7).

3. Giving Up Your Life for Your Love

This is self-sabotage at its best. Many grew up never feeling loved enough, encouraged, accepted, or cared for. These insecurities remain dormant in us for years. They manifest themselves in the form of blind love. When we even get a sense of love from someone, we get easily attached, as if we had never received love before. This is what happened to Nancy. She grew up with parents who always tried to discourage her from having a mind of her own.

Her thoughts about her life were not sinful; they just weren't familiar to them. They only encouraged her to do what they were used to. Why? They were used to keeping their fears and insecurities at bay. When Christ has called you to think higher, pursue higher, and go and live higher than the people that you love, **their anxieties are not your problem.** They must give their fears over to Jesus. I don't care whose life you become a part of; keep the life that the Lord Jesus has designed for you. Let's be clear: there's a difference between living your life and being stubborn.

We are supposed to love everyone, compromise in our marriages, be understanding but stern with our children, be open to new ideas from our colleagues, and consider the advice of our friends, but remain true to the truth of our Christ-ordained uniqueness. Hear me when I say that you are not called to worry about letting people down who were counting on you to keep the family business going, be like them, or live scared for the rest of your life. You are called to greatness.

Speaking of greatness, "Greater is He that is in you than he that is in the world" (1 John 4:4). Jesus promised his disciples that "I tell you the truth, anyone who believes in me will do the same works I have done, and even greater works, because I am going to be with the Father" (John 14:12, NLT).

4. Too Scared to Do Something New

Everyone in danger is not in an abusive relationship, protective custody, or suicide watch. The most dangerous place to be is where we play it safe. We have been hurt by so many bad experiences and people from the past that we decided to build a house out of someone else's home. We have decided to make peace with defeat and settle for someone who has already taken.

Although you may still be productive as far as going to work daily, raising the kids, and attending church weekly, there is something internally that you're suppressing that Jesus Christ has called you to do. As long as you sit on it, you will be unhappy, and there aren't enough sex, drugs, alcohol, fear, insecurity, or joy killers that can change that.

Jonah ran from his call and was miserable until he gave God total obedience as told in the Book of Jonah, chapters 1-4.

Our fear of trying something new has become so dangerous that we cuss anyone out who dare point out that we aren't living up to our Christ-given potential. We call them haters out of our insecurity because they dared to be honest and be the friend that the other friends in your life won't be, and that is a truth-teller.

Many have such strong insecurities that you'll take advice from a total stranger rather than those who care and love you to the degree to which they may even sound like an enemy to tell you the truth. Many of us cling to childhood information such as "You can't do anything besides clean," "You don't know how to take care of business," "You wouldn't last a day in the real world," "No man will put up with you." Clinging to this information will keep us in a chronic cycle of pain. Not another day, I say! Not another day!

That "You Complete Me" Speech is a Lie You Didn't Know You Were Telling

Jamie Foxx did his thing in the movie *Ray* (2004). A scene rings volumes to me that teaches a timely lesson. At seven years old, Ray is blind, and in this scene, he falls in the middle of the floor. His mother's reaction, at first, was to go and help him, but she had to remember what she told him when he was losing his sight: "Ok, I'll show you how to do something once. I'll help you if you mess up twice, but you're on your own the third time. Because that's the way it is in the world. Alright, now get up. Remember you going blind, but you ain't stupid."

Ray's mother might have sounded cruel, but that was the kindest thing anyone could ever say to the gifted Ray. He was looking for pity, and what he got was empowerment. He might have gotten sidetracked by heroin, multiple affairs, and unresolved grief from blaming himself for his brother's death. However, Ray never forgot what his mother told him. She wanted Ray to realize that he already had inside of him what being blind would tempt him to look for in other people. That's God's word to somebody reading this: You already have Jesus on the inside of you to do what you are looking for others to help you do.

I have heard many – especially women – tell their spouse or significant other, "You complete me." This is self-sabotage in a fairy-tale. When we don't realize that we don't love ourselves, we also don't know when we are subconsciously looking for other people to meet our needs. **It's a dangerous thing when we place our esteem and worth into the hands of someone else who is secretly trying to figure themselves out as well.**

It's a dangerous thing when we place our esteem and worth into the hands of someone else who is secretly trying to figure themselves out as well.

Our Insecurity Is Not Their Responsibility

One of the biggest recipes for heartbreak is to look for people to have your heart.

If you want to make somebody mad, take them at their word when they say they won't get mad. Many of us are frustrated when we aren't invited to certain events, aren't included in vacations, or are the last to know. We are mad at people for having a life. **One of the biggest recipes for heartbreak is to look for people to have your heart.** What do I mean? One of the ways we try to feel better about ourselves is by doing more for people just to win them over, in secret hopes that they will like us better.

Let's be honest; you can't even trust your own heart. The Bible made it clear that "the human heart is the most deceitful of all things, and desperately wicked. Who knows how bad it is?" (Jeremiah 17:9, NLT). Give people a break because they don't want the job of being our very own personal self-esteem assistant.

Self-Esteem vs. Christ-Esteem

That's the difference between self-confidence and Christ-confidence. Self-esteem often is not aware that we are trying to prove to others that we got this. The Christ-esteem mindset knows how to balance out needing Christ and when to depend on people some of the time. The Christ-confident person is not looking for others to be to them what only Christ Jesus can be. A Christ-esteem person live by the motto: Can't Nobody Do Me Like Jesus. Self-confident individuals do not isolate themselves from others, pretending "I don't need anyone." They have a balanced life.

Trying to Fit In Is the Reason Why You're Still Broken

Anyone who says they don't want to be liked is lying to themselves. We all want to be accepted and loved for who we are. God made us social creatures. Foxes turn to their holes. A bird can go to its nest. Humans have an innate desire to go to each other. We must have some kind of connection to feel secure. David knows what this feels like.

He never seemed to fit in around his own family. They misinterpreted his faith in God for arrogance (1 Samuel 17:24-31). David does not know how to be socially acceptable in the palace because most of his time has been spent in fields with sheep. David, however, is good at taking orders. He does whatever the King tells him to do. "Whatever Saul asked David to do, David did it successfully" (1 Samuel 18:5, NLT).

Being gifted does not bring confidence, nor does it replace confidence. One can be gifted, talented, anointed, and skilled and simultaneously feel unworthy and inadequate. David was gifted, talented, anointed, and skilled, but he could not seem to end the ongoing fight with not fitting in. Many of us have wasted time. We spend money, sweat, and tears trying to win the approval of someone or a group of people who may or may not like or accept us. Parents, it is important to teach your children to be ok with not being liked and accepted by everyone.

"Nobody Sees Me"

Beyond the Lights tells the story of a talented singer with a bright future of stardom, named Noni, played by Gugu Mabatha-Raw. She has been raised by a mother who has overly pushed her daughter to succeed. Noni can't seem to cope with the pressure of success, believing that she is loved for what she does and not who she is. The movie opens with her wanting to kill herself. Her bodyguard Kaz, played by Nate Parker, tries to talk her off the ledge; she makes a powerful statement to which we all can relate, at some point and time: "Nobody sees me." I want to outline three points to you with this movie in mind:

- The Stage Lights

The stage lights are where we hide the most. It is where we make others happy but suffer ourselves in silence. We are being what others want us to be because we just want to be loved and accepted. We are secretly carrying the regret of knowing that we are not keeping it real with ourselves. It is the place where we have some level of comfort in lying to ourselves. There's a saying that goes, "the most dangerous liars are the ones who think they are telling the truth."

Noni was being who her mother wanted her to be. Her mother asked her, rhetorically, "Do you want to be a runner up, or do you want to be a winner?" Her mother, like many parents, wanted her child to reach for the stars. However, her mother never told her it was ok to be who Christ wanted her to be. Let me tell you, the most dangerous thing we can do on stage is not let the light of Christ within not shine brighter than the stage lights we so desperately seek.

- Your Christ Given Light Within

> *"For God, who said, 'Let there be light in the darkness,' has made this light shine in our hearts so we could know the glory of God that is seen in the face of Jesus Christ. We now have this light shining in our hearts, but we are like fragile clay jars containing great treasure. This makes it clear that our great power is from God, not from ourselves" (2 Corinthians 4:6-7, NLT).*

The Apostle Paul reminds the baptized believer that we have the light of Christ inside of our fragile bodies. He makes it clear that this light has power because this light is the power of God. Yes, Jesus Christ is the power of God because he is God. Jesus Christ told us what to do with the light that he had placed inside of us when we obeyed the gospel, repented of our sins, and were baptized in water in the name of the Lord Jesus Christ (Acts 2:38). Christ tells us:

> *"13 "You are the salt of the earth. But what good is salt if it has lost its flavor? Can you make it salty again? It will be thrown out and trampled underfoot as worthless.14 "You are the light of the world—like a city on a hilltop that cannot be hidden. 15 No one lights a lamp and then puts it under a basket. Instead, a lamp is placed on a stand, giving light to everyone in the house. 16 In the same way, let your good deeds shine out for all to see so that everyone will praise your heavenly Father" (Matthew 5:13-16, NLT).*

Notice Christ clarifies that he has given us his eternal light, which is himself. Jesus said, "But while I am in the world, I am the light of the world" (John 9:5, NLT). See, we can dim the stage lights, but the cameraman cannot dim the eternal light of Christ inside you. You may backslide, but you can't seem to get away from that eternal light of Christ Jesus. Even the people you're sinning with can tell you to go to church. The Light of Christ will tell on you. Your low self-esteem cannot even dim the light. When Peter tried to deny that he was a disciple of Jesus Christ, someone pointed out the light of Christ was shining in his speech.

In my journey, I noticed that I was more frustrated when I tried to dim Christ's light because I did not want others to assume that I was arrogant. Arrogance is to trade your light of Christ for someone else's light is. Noni was shining, but it was not for Christ; she shined to make her mother happy. The conflict of interest for us is to love people but please Christ.

- **Backstage Darkness**

This is the real us. I call it backstage darkness because we have a part of our lives that we might have not shown family or close friends. Nevertheless, like Noni, if you're not yourself on stage with the stage lights, you'll continue to suffer backstage in the dark. The insecure, who cover their insecurities by acting like they have it all together, also cry in the dark. Christ Jesus, the light of the world, is calling you out of darkness into his marvelous light.

Noni felt that nobody noticed her. How can we be noticed for who we are if we're protecting someone else's ego by being who we are not? Many are in an abusive relationship, whether it be emotional, verbal, or physical. They have been manipulated into believing that they are worthless without their abuser and in the backstage darkness cage of fear and chronic anxiety. Jesus Christ is calling you out of the dark place today! God might have only wanted you to read this book for this part, but you *must* come out of that dark place.

Don't allow anyone to make you think that you're worthless without them. You were and still are somebody before you met them. Before you were formed in your mother's womb, God says he knew you (Jeremiah 1:5). You are called to reach others who are in the same darkness you faced, but you must know your worth is hidden only in Christ.

"My People Have Committed Two Evils"

It breaks the heart of God to see us frustrated, looking to get others to do what only Jesus Christ is God enough to do. "For my people have committed two evils; they have forsaken ME the fountain of living waters, and hewed them out cisterns that can hold no water" (Jeremiah 2:13)." I will never forget a good friend who is focused, accomplished and God-driven that fell in love with a woman who was not the best fit for him.

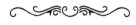

It breaks the heart of God to see us frustrated, looking to get others to do what only Jesus Christ is God enough to do.

He loved her, but she started giving him many symptoms. He began having chronic headaches, mood swings, and his work productivity fell tremendously. The most devastating statement that he made was, "I turned my back on God for her." That sent chills through my body. Thankfully, he left her and went back to walking in his God-ordained purpose. Please, whatever you do, don't forsake Christ to make anyone happy.

It will only feed your insecurities when you are chasing the wrong people. He described her as pretty, educated, and popular because he secretly felt average and unpopular. While you're judging him, pick yourself off the ground, wipe the

I refuse to lose my call over somebody who answered theirs. Now is a good time to remind you that you need Christ-confidence.

look of shock off your face, and think about the call and purpose that Christ has on your life that you have turned away from because you think you're too inadequate for. **To stay with God but run from the mandate and purpose he has given you is just as if you left him.** Nobody is that fine, gifted, popular, or anointed to turn your back on your purpose. **I refuse to lose my call over somebody who answered theirs. Now is** a good time to remind you that you need Christ-confidence.

Acting Out Is Acting Hurt

If we want to locate our confidence level, one great indicator is how we react. Our reactions indicate how much faith and confidence we have in Christ within us. Many of us carry suppressed rage, resentment, and regret because we have not dealt with those emotions from our childhood, past relationships, divorce, trauma, or present fears. Consequently, we act out when someone, something triggers us, or someplace that reminds us of our past. I call it acting hurt.

What do I mean? **One of the consequences of unhealthy self-esteem is the self-sabotage of acting out our pain in ways that place us and our fears in a compromising position.** Many who have a reputation for lashing

One of the consequences of unhealthy self-esteem is the self-sabotage of acting out our pain in ways that place us and our fears in a compromising position.

out, breaking windows, engaging in self-destructive behavior, and overindulgence are the manifestations of unhealed hurt that have weakened our self-worth. Some of us explode when we feel not heard, hurt, and frustrated.

Overreacting can make you look like a know-it-all who lashes out at others, trying to be the center of attention. We just want to be heard, but some of us get loud when we feel like nobody is listening, paying us any mind, or triggered by old past feelings by the present circumstances.

"I Don't Do Noise"

Everyone who battles with their self-esteem does not react loudly – others internalize, holding it in. We will never heal by hiding the wounds. However, the one who suffers in silence has made a false sense of peace with their insecurities. They are too embarrassed to verbalize their pain. These are the individuals who over-analyze everyone's actions and words.

Some people are not loud but may finally let it out on those who have anything to do with the source of their frustration. Or they can go off when treated in a way that resembles past treatment. In psychology, we call this displacement – one of the many defense mechanisms we use – when we are not dealing with the source of our frustration.

Thirty Minutes Before It's Over

"How many people are there?" "Fix me a to-go plate." "I'm not staying long." We have heard these comments before. Some of them we have said. We often sound antisocial or do not want to be bothered by people. However, it was said out of unhealthy self-worth when Beth said it.

Beth has battled with low self-esteem all her life due to a stuttering problem. No one in her family has tried to assist her in finding help. Beth is also unaware that others have been able to overcome their stutter.

Beth avoids attending events where she thinks she will be required to speak. By the way, Beth is a top leading neurologist. Remember, we stated earlier that situational self-esteem is very real. It is possible to be confident in one area but insecure in others. She is accomplished but believes her stutter dominates her success. She researches neurology to train her understudies. Still, she will not speak on her published journals or many other successes. She chooses to arrive late rather than to arrive confident in her craft.

Safe but Not Free

Anxiety is no joke. Fear is an ongoing battle, and PTSD is traumatizing. However, low self-esteem will ruin your whole life if you let it. Many of us choose safe situations, people we feel safe with, and levels we feel safe on to avoid feelings of low self-worth and live in a false sense of contentment. I have seen some friends and family stay in situations where they were not happy because they settled for safety. My mind was made up. I was determined that would not be me.

Love the people in your life and want the best for them, but do not forget your purpose or downplay it because they play games with theirs.

Listen, that's not arrogance; that Christ-confidence. **Love the people in your life and want the best for them, but do not forget your purpose or downplay it because they play games with theirs.** You cannot

afford to waste another day settling for anything less than what Christ Jesus has placed you on this earth for.

Self-Confidence VS Christ-Confidence

A self-confident person observes how they react to situations. They think before they speak without saying everything that they think. They have learned the difference between reacting and responding. They have bigger things to do than leave a comment on the status of every negative critic around them. They have learned to stop majoring in the minor.

A Christ-confident individual knows the power of letting Christ be their peace. A Christ-confident individual understands that the enemy cannot attack them without God's permission. They aren't angry with God about that because they have flood insurance. They know that "when the enemy shall come in like a flood, the spirit of the Lord shall lift a standard Against him" (Isaiah 59:19). A Christ-confident individual knows that they can get the last word out of their self-confidence, but they choose to let Christ be their anchor because of their Christ -Confidence.

The Sin of Self-Sabotage That We Won't Repent

Many presumptuously assume that the only sins that require repentance are clubbing, drinking, getting high, adultery, or homosexuality. However, in the eyes of Christ, "All unrighteousness is sin" (1 John 5:17). Furthermore, there is a sin that we don't discuss, which is self-sabotage. We marry people we don't love, but we don't want to be alone. We took toxicity that God told us not to enter, but misery loves company. We went back to who Christ pulled us away from because we miss them more than we do our future. You may not repent for theft, murder, or hatred. However, we must repent for settling for less than Christ has for us. Don't you realize that Christ can do exceedingly, abundantly, above all we ask or think (Ephesians 3:20)? One of the primary reasons many believers backslide is due to the fact that we have taught people to be holy but not Christ-confident. Remember, I stated earlier that people go back to what makes them feel good about themselves. So many are holy (baptized in the name of the Lord Jesus Christ and filled with the Holy Spirit) but aren't walking in the peace of God that surpasses all understanding.

Forgive Yourself for Settling

Believe it or not, it is possible to spend many years of our lives in church settling. It happens every Sunday. I get more phone calls from people settling in a church God has called them out of, but they don't want to hurt the pastor's feelings. God has called them into a new office, but they do not want to offend the board of bishops who bailed their child out of jail. I have also seen individuals settle for positions God never gave them. Still, they didn't know how to say no out of fear and embarrassment of being disobedient to the leader.

Maybe you weren't settling in Church but chose not to take the promotion because you don't want to face the pressure of keeping up with everyone else. Or you settle for the man that was available because your biological clock was ticking, and you didn't want to be viewed as the last one to get married. Maybe you feel like you have to walk on eggshells around the people you love, suppressing your passion because your dreams and goals don't resemble theirs.

I think it's about time you disappoint some people so that you won't miss your appointment with your purpose.

How can you be unique if you live in constant fear of disappointing those who you love? **I think it's about time you disappoint some people so that you won't miss your appointment with your purpose.**

> [5] *Trust in the* LORD *with all thine heart; and lean not unto thine own understanding.* [6] *In all thy ways acknowledge him, and he shall direct thy paths. (Proverbs 3:5-6).*

PART 3

Soul Snatcher

CHAPTER FIVE

Lonely Faith

"I don't mind when you say that you're going
away; I just don't want to be lonely."
—Cuba Gooding Sr. & the Main Ingredient

"You're a good man, and I'm a lonely woman. That's a bad combination." Those were the words of a woman who was the secretary to her boss who came over to her apartment one night because he felt neglected and unappreciated by his wife of seventeen years. She was very much into him. She would even fantasize about him in her dreams. She engaged in personal conversations with him about things she would not want her man to discuss with the opposite sex. Do we give her a break? After all, she was lonely.

He was a hard-working man who owned a car dealing business. He was a father of six and did his very best to make his wife happy, though she could not seem to be satisfied. **A good man is not himself when he**

A good man is not himself when he doesn't feel appreciated. A good woman feels things she doesn't want to feel when lonely.

doesn't feel appreciated. **A good woman feels things she doesn't want to feel when lonely.** He wasn't alone, but he felt lonely. There is a difference between alone and lonely. Both individuals had a need, but only one had a secret. Both wanted each other's company, but only one of them was married. Both needed someone to talk to, but only one had a spouse he could vent to.

That's the issue with co-dependency. It's one-sided. It can also be life-threatening for individuals with low self-esteem. Not having the courage to go to the person they are with might make them vulnerable to anyone who seems accepting, non-judgmental, forgiving, and available to them. Alternatively, the single secretary may continue to entertain a married man because she allows him to make her feel good about herself. It's one-sided.

I Need Jesus, but I Want You

"She's gotta have it." You've heard that expression before, right? Let me correct that. For one, it's more than sex. It sometimes entails wanting what and who is not yours. Sometimes it's trying to make a house out of someone else's home. Sometimes, it's trying to make someone stay with you who already verbalized that they want to go. Sometimes, it's spying on the Facebook page of someone who blocked you from another page.

Sometimes it's the motive behind the need that causes the problems. **We all have needs, but not all people can supply our needs. That's where Christ comes**

We all have needs, but not all people can supply our needs. That's where Christ comes in.

in. Many of us are frustrated because we have failed in our attempts to persuade others to be who only Christ can be. We say, "Jesus is my doctor," for instance, but we still go back to the individual that makes us sick. God has given you someone who will assist you in instilling mental and emotional wellness. At the same time, we continue to tolerate those who make us sick. Yes, loneliness is real.

Lonesome vs Lonely

Dr Gary Chapman, the author of the New York Times best-selling book, *The Five Love Languages,* defines the difference between being lonesome and lonely. "Lonesome is when somebody is not there, and you know they will be back after a while. Being lonely is when you don't have anybody to be lonesome for" (One More Try, p. 96). Sometimes we hold conversations with people we wouldn't normally talk to, sleep with people we would not marry, and entertain toxic friendships out of fear of being alone or the misery of feeling lonely.

Being alone is hard for many of us, but it is a challenge for those who battle low self-esteem. Being alone is when it's time to face things we have been running from and trying the hardest to ignore. Inside the insecure mind, being alone is an indictment of their self-worth. We all want to be loved but don't want to be alone while waiting for that special someone.

Who Told You You're Alone?

Janet was a 36-year-old pediatrician who was successful with no kids. However, she battles with low self-esteem. Why would a successful woman, who is used to getting attention from men, educated, and family-oriented feel insecure? We would have to get that answer from her mother.

Janet's mother constantly drilled in her daughter's head that all her accomplishments are useless without a man. She was conditioned to believe what her mother told her. We cannot, however, just look at her mother. The society around her, which entails tv shows, magazines, Instagram, Facebook, confirms her mother's teaching that she is inadequate without a man. Therefore, here are some things to remember for many of us who think being in a relationship will be the cure to our loneliness:

- A relationship will not always make us feel loved and wanted
- A relationship does not always guarantee that we will live happily ever after
- A relationship will not give us true esteem (Christ-confidence)
- A relationship does not define our worth.
- Being in a relationship should complement the Christ-confidence we already have
- Using a relationship to cover up low self-esteem is a recipe for disaster. We must have Christ-confidence before a relationship instead of looking for it in another person once we are in the middle of a relationship
- Staying in the wrong relationship or staying for the wrong reasons is mentally, emotionally, spiritually, and physically disastrous.
- Staying in the wrong relationship will often end in us losing our sense of worth
- Begging someone to stay who made it clear, through actions and words, they don't want to stay, will do more damage to our sense of worth and have us mistreating the ones who came to love us correctly

How Single Are You?

That is the question today in the dating game? Back in the day, we took someone at their word when they told us they were single. Today, we have to ask, "Are you single, single?" "Do you have someone sliding in your DM's?" "Do you have someone living with you in the next room?" When people get frustrated with these questions, something is not right. What is the purpose of getting to know someone if we cannot ask questions? Many of us are embarrassed to be alone because we lived in social culture and were brought up in a family that made us believe that we are incomplete without someone.

It's Not You; It's Us

If the truth is told, a true sign of a healthy relationship is letting the one you love have their space. Let's be clear: there is a difference between secrecy and privacy. We all are entitled to have time to ourselves, even if we have a significant other. Nevertheless, it's dangerous to spend too much time alone. The word of Christ cautions married couples not to spend too much time away, even sexually, because it will give the enemy room to occupy space in a union that God put together (1 Corinthians chapter 7).

It's hard to admit to people who would have never hurt us that we have hurt them.

In substance abuse counseling, one of the hardest things to assist clients with is admitting to their loved ones that they have been using them (manipulating them to cater to their habit or using love to con their loved ones after being confronted about their behavior). **It's hard to admit to**

people who would have never hurt us that we have hurt them. It adds insult to injury that we used them to cure our loneliness and fragile egos.

Sorensen states, "healthy relationships are ones in which both partners are healthy individuals or individuals striving to become healthier and who have interests, goals, friends, activities, and a sense of worth not related to their partner. Just as a chain can be no greater than its weakest link, so too a relationship can only be as healthy as its least healthy member" (Sorensen, pg. 162).

Family Matters

The '90s were a great era. One of the things that made the 90's great for me was the television shows that had a message to them. *Family Matters* was one of them. It was a show about a middle-class family who is close to each other and embraces family values. You could tell when the show was about to be over because the music would play softly in the background when a lesson was about to be given on life.

Three characters that gave the show some spice were Laura Winslow, played by Kellie Shanygne Williams-Jackson. We cannot forget the talented Jaleel White, who played Steve Urkel. Urkel was highly infatuated with Laura, who made it very clear in her words and actions that she could not stand Steve, nor did she like him "like that." Steve was clumsy, full of life, and what others would call a nerd. Laura would rather be alone than be caught with Steve regardless of how nice he was. Then came Stephon.

Steve was an inventor. So, he transforms himself into Laura's dream guy. Laura was in love with Stephon that Steve would transform himself into instead of who he was as a person. Some might say that that show was exaggerating, but we all have felt like Steve. Despite our talents, good hearts, and capabilities, there will always be some people who will not be impressed. The irony is that Urkel had a girlfriend who loved him for every part of himself.

If someone is trying to manipulate you, change everything about you, what about you do they like? Everything Steve wanted in Laura; he already had it in Myra. The only problem is that everything he had in Myra he did not have in himself. I want to pause and make two points about the loneliness of being alone:

If someone is trying to manipulate you, change everything about you, what about you do they like?

1. If we are coupled with someone who does not allow or embrace who we are, we will constantly feel alone. This is where setting boundaries is pivotal. We must know who we are in Christ; getting our confidence in him before looking for confidence in someone else is everything to the wellness of our Souls.

2. Loneliness will always be there when we are not our Christ-given selves. As one wise woman stated in the movie, *A Rage in Harlem,* "If you could afford love, Jesus wouldn't have had to go to Calvary."

Cheating

Let's clear the myth that we cheat because we aren't getting what we want out of our relationship or marriage. Let's take away the pop-culture theory that we cheat because we aren't getting what we need at home. While these may be contributing factors, they are not the driving forces that make one cheat. However, allow me to address one of many factors listed for cheating. Interestingly, it has nothing to do with their spouse. It's boredom.

"Boredom kills," they say. However, the question arises: How can we be bored with ourselves when Christ has already uniquely made us in His image? We are what the Bible calls the apple of God's eye (Deuteronomy 32:10). How can we get bored with our gifted selves? How can we get bored when we are who Christ Jesus says we are? I want to introduce four primary reasons why being alone is challenging for many of us:

1. Being Alone Means I Have to Face Myself

Sadly, many of us have used others to cure our loneliness, whether we want to admit it or not. Even those who aren't particularly fond of company have benefited from entertaining someone they wouldn't tolerate on a good day. One of the most challenging things to confront when we are by ourselves is admitting that we have not finished what we have started; we have let ourselves and others down; we have deep-seated pain, trauma, and hurt that we have avoided by staying in the crowds.

There are some mothers, for example, who had used their son as a boyfriend when their father walked away. This is what I call "emotional incest." We often reduce incest to sexual relationships between family members. However, we have forgotten the pleasure and connection many get from emotional incest.

Even in Church, many join multiple committees to avoid the loneliness they feel inside. When someone in the committee hurts their feelings, they take it very personally.

There are some marriages where one spouse may stay at work longer. The boss has given raises for their hard work and dedication for being "the first one to come and the last one to leave." However, the boss is not mindful that the hard-working employee might not be so dedicated if they did not feel lonely.

That's the danger of a one-sided affair. That individual you are sleeping with may give you sex, but it's only because they want company. Others might even go as far as being seen with you in public or even invite you to family events. You may think this is someone you want to spend the rest of your life with. However, the family is giving funny looks because they know that it won't be long before she does to you what she does to the rest of her other men. Fellas, we are not exempt. If you feel alone in your marriage, you won't fix it by sleeping with the girl next door.

2. Not Knowing What Our Purpose, Calling, and Gifts Are

We all have people that we admire. Nothing is wrong with that if we admire them for the right reasons. **Nevertheless, many of us admire people because we secretly like them. After all, we believe they have what we don't or are what we aren't.** Hear me out: No one is so good at what they do that they can do what Jesus Christ has called you to do. And I mean absolutely, positively on one! Growing up, I saw great, dynamic preachers around me, some of whom I wanted to emulate.

Nevertheless, many of us admire people because we secretly like them. After all, we believe they have what we don't or are what we aren't.

God reminded me that the style and anointing he placed on my life was enough for what he has called me to do. We must embrace who we are in Christ, and we must also embrace who we are not! Whoever you are in Christ is more than a conqueror (Romans 8:37). When we know our Christ-given uniqueness, we don't mind celebrating the uniqueness of others. That brings me back to King David and King Saul's jealous rivalry.

> *1-3 Saul called his son Jonathan together with his servants and ordered them to kill David. But because Jonathan treasured David, he went and warned him: "My father is looking for a way to kill you. Here's what you are to do. Tomorrow morning, hide and stay hidden. I'll go out with my father into the field you are hiding. I'll talk about you with my father, and we'll see what he says. Then I'll report back to you." 4-5 Jonathan brought up David with his father, speaking well of him. "Please," he said to his father, "don't attack David. He hasn't wronged you, has he? And just look at all the good he has done! He put his life on the line when he killed the Philistine. What a great victory GOD gave Israel that day! You were there. You saw it and were on your feet, applauding with everyone else. So why would you even think of sinning against an innocent person, killing David for no reason whatever? (1 Samuel 19:1-5, MSG).*

King Saul did not mind celebrating King David until he forgot what God called him to do in moments of jealousy.

We must watch out for jealousy within, for jealousy is the son and daughter of low self-esteem. We often define praising God for what he has done for us already in the church world. However, I would like you to know that real worship is when we can thank God and be comfortable in our skin for who he created us to be! King Saul had a hard time praising God for who God is, fighting David for who David is because he couldn't focus on who he was. Read that again slowly! Baby, the best way to get over jealousy and walk in your Christ-confidence is to praise God for who you are and who you're not while trusting him to perfect the things that concern us (Psalms 138:6).

Many of us spend ample private time watching, mimicking, and trying to emulate those we admire. There was an episode of the television sitcom *Sister, Sister*, where Tia and Tamera were excited about their school prom. The big question of the day, though, was what gown to buy. Luckily, Tia's adopted mother, Lisa Landry, had a Fashion business called *With Lisa*. She made two gowns for her daughters, but they were not impressed. That broke Lisa's heart.

Tia and Tamera wanted to wear the dresses they thought would turn heads at the prom. Surprisingly, when they arrived at the prom, the room was filled with other girls who had gowns they thought would also make them stand out. Ironically, Lisa saved the day. She told the girls that she still had the gowns she designed for them that they originally did not want in the car's back seat. They were elated.

When they walked into the room with the gowns designed by Lisa, the atmosphere shifted. They were happy. The moral of the story is the twins did not value their uniqueness because they thought it was mediocre. Being alone is time to focus on your unique gifts rather than live in the shadow of someone else's success.

32 "Master," said David, "don't give up hope. I'm ready to go and fight this Philistine."33 Saul answered David, "You can't go and fight this Philistine. You're too young and inexperienced—and he's been at this fighting business since before you were born."34-37 David said, "I've been a shepherd, tending sheep for my father. Whenever a lion or bear came and took a lamb from the flock, I'd go after it, knock it down, and rescue the lamb. If it turned on me, I'd grab it by the throat, wring its neck, and kill it. Lion or bear, it made no difference—I killed it. And I'll do the same to this Philistine pig who is taunting the troops of God-Alive. GOD, who delivered me from the teeth of the lion and the claws of the bear, will deliver me from this Philistine." Saul said, "Go. And GOD help you!" (1 Samuel 17:32-37, MSG).

Like King Saul, many who battle insecurities are so focused on coping with their fears and anxieties that they haven't given their gifts and talents any consideration. Or, if they did, they are quickly overwhelmed by the thoughts of something going wrong. If you ask them, "What's the worst that can happen," they have an answer for a plethora of things to list. David had time alone! Like a shepherd, God gave him an experience with a lion and a bear.

That gave him the Christ-confidence to know the same Jesus back then is the same God right now! Yes! "Jesus Christ, yesterday, today, and forever" (Hebrews 13:8). David realized that everything he went through in isolation confirmed his current situation! David was convinced, but Saul wasn't.

Hand-Me-Downs

Hand-me-downs are a colloquialism to describe clothes that others no longer want or don't fit any longer, so they hand it down to siblings, friends, or strangers. Then there is the hand-me-down of mixed messages that we have received from family growing up that has affected how we go after our dreams and goals today. Some of us might have come from families of well-meaning parents who told us to push towards our goals, but when we specified our goals, they were instantly shot down because our dream did not look like anything to them.

> *"38-39 Then Saul outfitted David as a soldier in armor. He put his bronze helmet on his head and belted his sword over the armor. David tried to walk, but he could hardly budge. David told Saul, "I can't even move with all this stuff on me. I'm not used to this." And he took it all off.40 Then David took his shepherd's staff, selected five smooth stones from the brook, and put them in the pocket of his shepherd's pack, and with his sling in his hand approached Goliath. (1 Samuel 17:38-40, MSG).*

David quickly learned that everyone who loves us couldn't help us if they didn't see what Christ Jesus had shown us. David had lonely faith. He learned what he could do for God when nobody else was looking, and he was determined to live for God – killing Goliath if no one showed up. Saul meant no harm in giving David his armor. After all, it was the king's armor; nevertheless, David knew that his help was in the name of the Lord Jesus (Psalms 124:8).

3. Guilt Is Felt Stronger When We Are Alone

Guilt is something those with low self-esteem know too well. Where there is a plethora of guilt in someone's heart, there is also the need for pleasing people. When we are plagued with the insecurity of guilt, we will notice that we will have people surrounding us who are skilled at making us feel guilty for doing what the LORD has put in our hearts. Hear me when I say this: **You will always end up smothering the ones you want to please while feeling miserable in the process.**

You will always end up smothering the ones you want to please while feeling miserable in the process.

4. Going Solo

I strongly believe that one of the primary reasons many fear being alone is that we cannot survive without some people. **Whoever you think you can't live without might be able to live without you. Never give someone the responsibility for validating your existence in this world.** There are some women, for instance, who know exactly what I am talking about, that has been with a controlling man for so long (who is fueled by his insecurities and anxieties) has been pre-programmed to only cling to men who make her feel like she should go against her

Whoever you think you can't live without might be able to live without you. Never give someone the responsibility for validating your existence in this world.

wants for him. It takes time to walk alone without what we've been used to, depending on the nods and approval of others.

Christ Likes Visiting You When You're By Yourself

When two people love each other, they want to be alone. Now there is a balance to this. Some are territorial – only wanting you to themselves to have control over you to soothe their insecurities. This happens countless times in relationships. Some men who have been abandoned have brainwashed a woman into disowning her own family to prove that she is committed to him. They even made a television show out of this concept called *For My Man.*

This show was about men battling insecurities that connect with women who also battle insecurities. In the end, they talk the woman into committing crimes for their man. This also happens to some women as well. Countless betrayals, being cheated on and lied to by men, some have become controlling, not wanting that man to have any friends. **Now is a good time to tell you everyone who clings to us doesn't love us.** It's true what they say, "Some people aren't looking for love; they're looking for help."

Now is a good time to tell you everyone who clings to us doesn't love us.

Some people only connect with us to get their needs met through us. When we meet people, we must decipher if they want to know us or just what we do. Additionally, I want you to keep in mind that sometimes the only thing someone may have in common is our insecurities. This often happens with the good girl, an internally broken girl who has a thing for bad boys. The good girl here wants a man who can give her the love, attention, and security she never had, but the nurturing part of her thinks she can fix him.

I will never forget a friend who came from the foster care system. She bounced from house to house. By the time she was twenty-four, she had already been through a myriad of failed relationships and drug addiction from city to city. Ultimately, she met a man who she thought was the one. I asked her what key feature qualified him to be the one. She stated, "We have so much in common." The only thing they had in common was low self-worth. It pays to know your worth. If all you have in common is the brokenness you call a connection, **you will need more repairs than remodels.** Both of you must come to Jesus Christ because he is the only one that can heal the brokenhearted, according to Luke 4:18.

You will need more repairs than remodels.

I promise you there's a friend in Jesus. He will wipe your tears away. I know you're afraid to be alone, but that's when Christ shows up the most.

> *"24 This left Jacob all alone in the camp, and a man came and wrestled with him until the dawn began to break. 25 When the man saw that he would not win the match, he touched Jacob's hip and wrenched it out of its socket. 26 Then the man said, "Let me go, for the dawn is breaking!" But Jacob said, "I will not let you go unless you bless me."27 "What is your name?" the man asked. He replied, "Jacob."28 "Your name will no longer be Jacob," the man told him. "From now on, you will be called Israel,[a] because*

you have fought with God and with men
and have won." (Genesis 32-24-28, NLT).

Now let's grab a few gems from the above passage.

Gem #1 – Jacob doesn't waste isolation.

Jacob had recently been married. He is now a father. He has a long-time family feud with his brother, Esau, but he is not alone. He has people in his life and out of his life. Jacob has spent time with everyone, including God. However, God wanted to hang out with Jacob again. Why? God revealed himself to Jacob a few chapters back (Genesis 28). This time God wants to reveal someone else to Jacob that he never had a chance to meet: Israel.

Jacob, in Hebrew, means *cunning*; Israel, in Hebrew, means *prince*. God is not trying to create a new Jacob; God introduces Jacob to Israel inside of him. The Bible never said if any man is in Christ, he is a better person. The Bible teaches that "If any man is in Christ, he is a *new creature* and behold all things have *become new* (2 Corinthians 5:17). We struggled with the word better in our insecurities while Jacob was wrestling with God for God to reveal what was new!

Jacob didn't waste this moment! He was not feeling sorry for himself. He refused to let guilt hold him and take away this precious interaction with the Father. He was simply looking up to Jesus, the author, and finisher of his faith, according to Hebrews 12:2.

Gem #2 – God knew who Jacob needed to be.

He needed to know who God wanted him to be so he could stop being who others called him. The God who knows all things asked a man, who only knew his flaws, "What is your name" (Genesis 32:27, NLT)? God got Jacob by himself to reveal to Jacob who he was in the kingdom. Many of us have a hard time being alone because we don't know how to answer the question, "Who are you?" We only socialize with those we think can answer that question for us even when they are toxic to us. Jacob was toxic to some people in his life because he was not aware there was a prince inside of him.

Maybe you're still begging a man to leave his wife, holding on to the false hope of his lies because you aren't mindful of the fact that there is a queen inside of you. Maybe you allow women to degrade you and even physically abuse you (yes, men go through domestic violence as well) because you don't know there is a king inside of you. You thought you were just reading this book to support me or purchase for someone you thought needed it. God has you surrounded! Lift your hands right now and ask the Lord Jesus to show you who you are!

The bottle of alcohol can't tell you. Another sex toy won't satisfy an identity crisis, and

neither will that escape you run to, hoping to numb the childhood pain you've suppressed. Come to Jesus. Come without money. Come without support. Come to Jesus without friends. Come to Jesus even in loneliness. If you can't get to him, ask him to come to you! He is an omnipresent God! Yes, Jesus Christ is Emmanuel (God with us), and He is the Holy Ghost (God in us).

The Urgency of Being Alone

Dr William D. Watley said it best, "You have to face it to fix it." I've seen men fight five guys at once but could not face themselves. I've seen the sassy girl on the block have multiple street fights but was scared to face herself. I've seen others who were very street smart at figuring out those around them but could not face themselves. We are afraid to confront ourselves because we have so many hurtful memories we have ignored, feelings of not being good enough, and disloyal people who we did not dismiss soon enough. If we avoid this, we aren't allowing Christ to heal us internally.

Until we embrace the urgency of being alone, we will not learn our strength in God; we will be constantly frustrated at those who can't spend the night, live recklessly, and ruin every good moment coming our way. Being alone is something that enhances the Christ-confidence in us. Until we understand that there are some places in our lives that Christ will take us, that some family and friends can't even fathom, understand, or go to, we will constantly be angry when our tactics to manipulate do not work.

Are you Still Awake?

"36-38 Then Jesus went with them to a garden called Gethsemane and told his disciples, "Stay here while I go over there and pray." Taking along Peter and the two sons of Zebedee, he plunged into an agonizing sorrow. Then he said, "This sorrow is crushing my life out. Stay here and keep vigil with me."39 Going a little ahead, he fell on his face, praying, "My Father, if there is any way, get me out of this. But please, not what I want. You, what do you want?"40-41 When he returned to his disciples, he found them sound asleep. He said to Peter, "Can't

you stick it out with me a single hour? Stay
alert; be in prayer so you don't wander into
temptation without even knowing you're in
danger. A part of you is eager, ready for any-
thing in God. But there's another part that's
as lazy as an old dog sleeping by the fire."⁴²
He then left them a second time. Again,
he prayed, "My Father, if there is no other
way than this, drinking this cup to the
dregs, I'm ready. Do it your way."⁴³⁻⁴⁴ When
he returned, he again found them sound
asleep. They simply couldn't keep their eyes
open. He let them sleep on this time and
went back a third time to pray, going over
the same ground one last time.⁴⁵⁻⁴⁶ When he
came back the next time, he said, "Are you
going to sleep on and make a night of it?
My time is up, the Son of Man is about
to be handed over to the hands of sinners.
Get up! Let's get going! My betrayer is here"
(Matthew 26:36-46, MSG).

Jesus is God, who manifested Himself in the flesh,
according to 1 Timothy 3:16). While He was in the flesh,
He felt everything we felt. The Bible says that our feelings
can touch Jesus because he can also be touched by feelings
(Hebrews 4:15-16). He knew what loneliness felt like. In the
above passage, Jesus Christ is coming close to completing his
mission of dying on the cross to save us from sin and death.
The closer He comes to set us free, humanity kicks in.

Jesus is in agony. Just the thought of having nails rushed
through his chest, the wood of the cross rubbing against his
beaten, bloody back of open wounds, and feeling abandoned

by God, is feeling anxiety like never before. Jesus wants to go into the garden of Gethsemane to pray.

Christ takes three of his twelve and asks them to go with him to pray. They fell asleep while he was praying to God. Because Jesus was God in a human body, he felt the pain that humans face. Here are some nuggets to take away from this powerful scene in the above passage.

1. Don't allow everyone into your Gethsemane.

Gethsemane is the place where our will dies, and we submit our will to the will of God. It is the place where we trade our confidence for the confidence of Christ. It's the place where we fight not to call ex-lovers, go back to old places, and leave our old habits. When we know who we are in Jesus Christ or want to know who we are in him, we go to Gethsemane even when others fall asleep.

2. Don't go through Gethsemane alone.

There are some Gethsemane moments in my life that I know I would not have made it through without the prayers of my grandmother, mom, pastor, and close friends. One of the most dangerous things to do is go through trouble in the church by yourself. Many of us come to church and tell each other that we are fine while fighting children on drugs, a broken marriage, and secret sins. Gethsemane is where you said, "Lord Jesus, I miss them, but help me not want it." Gethsemane is where you get to a place where you stop fighting with God. Gethsemane is where you fight to forgive the uncle that molested you or the father that never showed up for your games. Many of us are suffering in silence, which only intensifies the agony. Jesus, who did not need anyone, knew the importance of having someone to talk to outside of God.

3. Let them sleep.

Gethsemane is the only place where Jesus' disciples couldn't stay up with him through his agony. Jesus explained to them how he felt: *'This sorrow is crushing my life out. Stay here and keep vigil with me.'* Nevertheless, he finds them asleep while he prays. He even asked and told Peter, the one who promised to even die for Jesus, *He said to Peter, 'Can't you stick it out with me a single hour? Stay alert; be in prayer so you don't wander into temptation without even knowing you're in danger.*

They also slept because they were sorrowful, too (Luke 22:45). It looked like they did not care, but they handled their sorrow by sleeping. One of the symptoms of depression is sleeping more or less than usual. We often feel alone when our spouses, family, or friends don't worry the way we do or show outward signs of concern. Nevertheless, the Bible says while the disciples slept, God sent an angel (Luke 22:43). For every Gethsemane moment of our lives, God will always have an angel. Let them sleep. Jesus got strength from the angel and told the disciples to sleep on (Matthew 26:45).

Do You Know Your Strength?

If the disciples had not slept on Jesus, he would not have encountered the strength from the angel. Often, the people who sleep on us cause us to encounter our strength. How? As long as we allow insecurity to get in the way, we will never encounter our strength. King David knows exactly what I am talking about. It was his enemies that helped him to encounter his strength.

> *"The LORD is my light and my salvation; whom shall I fear? The LORD is the strength of my life; of whom shall I be afraid?² When the wicked, even mine enemies and my foes, came upon me to eat up my flesh, they stumbled and fell.³ Though a host should encamp against me, and my heart shall not fear: though war should rise against me, in this will I be confident"* (Psalms 27:1-3, KJV).

One of the signs of low self-worth is putting our strength in things or people that break us. David could throw a rock like nobody's business, but his confidence was not in his sling shot swag. David was successful in war, but he did not put his self-worth in his war skills. The king had already acknowledged,

One of the signs of low self-worth is putting our strength in things or people that break us.

with confidence, "Blessed be the LORD, my rock, who trains my hands for war, and my fingers for battle" (Psalms 144:1).

David teaches us that the best way to fight insecurities is to fight them with confidence in Christ.

When we put our confidence in who and what we think made us, it breeds self-confidence. The danger about putting too much confidence in self is that humans make mistakes. Humans fail. Humans with only humanity feel empty inside. Please don't get me started on placing confidence in people to decide our worth. Let's be clear I'm not speaking of healthy confidence in a wife or husband, children, or those we have a close connection with. I'm talking about when we allow them to decide who we are – that's too much confidence and rights to hand over to others that can only be handed down from Christ.

Being Alone Doesn't Cost a Thing

In the movie *Love Don't Cost a Thing,* Nick Cannon plays Alvin Johnson. Many consider Alvin the unpopular kid in high school who is extremely gifted at fixing cars. The only problem is he can't seem to fit his perception of himself. Often when we can't fix our insecurities on the inside, we try to fix the outside. Others overuse their gift to compensate for their lack of people skills. The man who doesn't know how to be intimate or communicate will try to hide that with his sexual performance, wondering why women only call him over when they want to have sex.

Subsequently, Alvin is attracted to Christina Milian, who plays Paris Morgan. He wants to get with her, but he knows he doesn't stand a chance because he is not the typical guy she would date. She dates popular guys, not nerds. Plus, she is already taken, but her boyfriend is away while her car needs to be repaired. The repairs cost $1,500, and as a high school student, Paris doesn't have that kind of money. This appears to be Alvin's time to slide in and get what he wants out of the deal.

Despite her not having the money, he offers to fix her car if she dates him for two weeks. She reluctantly agrees to it. However, this messy drama takes an unexpected shift midway into the movie. Alvin begins to get arrogant. Now he thinks he is God's gift to women. Also, Paris's boyfriend returns. He finds out she is dating Alvin. He is insulted that she was messing around on him with a nerd. She has a self-esteem attack, knowing that he could leave her.

Next, she runs to Alvin to speak to the boyfriend to explain that what they were doing was only a business transaction. Alvin does not want to do it. She tells him, "I made you Al, and I can break you." By the end of the movie, Paris realizes she loves Alvin and consequently leaves her boyfriend. This takes place after Alvin expressed to her and the crowd that listened to him at the basketball games that he finally accepts himself for who he is. Alvin realized love doesn't cost a thing.

Now that sounds like a cute love story, but the counselor and preacher in me have stood up to say, "Not so fast!" There are some major lessons that this movie teaches us that we can take nuggets from.

1 – She already has a boyfriend.

The danger of using a relationship to heal our insecurities does not work. Yes, Paris is good-looking, popular, and all the guys want her. They say, "Everyone wants who they can't have." Others say, "After you get into a relationship, everybody wants you." This is just life. However, I don't want what everyone can have, and you shouldn't either. Suppose someone agrees to talk to you, knowing that you are already in a relationship. In that case, they don't respect the person they are with, and they won't respect you. More importantly, it shows you don't allow yourself enough time to respect yourself. You are not a disappointment because you're alone.

2 – Don't sell your soul for company.

The moment we allow people to place a price on our worth, they take all the profits. One of the major differences between being self-confident and Christ-confident is that individuals don't know the full amount of their worth. Christ-confident individuals realize that God loved them so

The moment we allow people to place a price on our worth, they take all the profits.

much that he wrapped himself up in the flesh and came to earth and purchased us with His blood. Yes, He valued us so much that money was beneath him. It took the currency of the blood of Christ. Stop allowing others to take you to the bargain basement just because you haven't felt like yourself lately.

3 – Spend time alone after a break-up.

This is a fight for most of us but a chronic fight for those with low self-esteem. They may feel like a nobody without somebody. Maybe someone verbally and physically abused you, telling you that you're nothing without them and no one but them would ever put it with you.

Then that person who told us those things leaves us. That's enough to make anyone feel alone and lonely. He accepted himself, and now he has to give her time to accept herself. If we love someone, we must let Christ heal them while supporting them.

The Balance between Extraversion and Introversion

In western culture, extroverts are seen as more socially and mentally well. In contrast, introverts are viewed as if there is something wrong. Let's be clear: Introverts are not always timid, shy, sociopaths, or anti-social. Extraverts are not always the healthiest. Sometimes it could be attention-seeking. Neither personality is wrong; they are just different. So, let's distinguish between Introverts and Extroverts:

Introverts:

- Need time alone to process their thoughts
- They prefer to exercise alone
- They do like to talk to a degree; only to those they feel comfortable with

Extroverts:

- Think out loud. They don't need to process. They speak their mind.
- They are stimulated by crowds, events, and being with others.
- They deal with despair, sadness, and betrayal by socializing with others.

When an introvert has low self-worth, it adds another layer to their introversion. An introvert with low self-worth isolates way too much. They stay home when dealing with loss, marital issues, occupational problems, and rejection. They will go MIA (Missing in Action) without warning and get upset when confronted. Just because an introverted child likes to be alone does not mean he has low self-esteem. However, if that child, who was once the life of the party, shutdowns out of nowhere, then that can be a concern.

The introvert with low self-worth is notorious for sending mixed signals. They like being alone but don't want to be alone. However, when they see someone who they think can cure their loneliness, they may even appear to come off as extroverted to get their attention and win them over. Nevertheless, they may go to their room and stay there for hours once they get them.

When the extrovert confronts them, telling them they have been very distant, they respond with, "What are you talking about? I'm fine."

The extrovert, on the other hand, with low self-esteem, hates silence with a passion. They will break up with you for not responding to a text in five minutes. They feel isolated without someone. They are only comfortable in a relationship where they make their significant other believe they must do everything together. A true sign of a healthy relationship is allowing others to have their space. Extroverts, who battle with low self-esteem, can drain others who don't always feel like talking on the phone or wanting company. They have not learned that a relationship doesn't heal the wounds on the inside.

Self-Confidence vs. Christ-Confidence for the Extrovert & Introvert

Introverts with low self-worth must realize that they don't have to go through everything independently. The only problem with being self-sufficient is that we might reject the people Jesus Christ has placed into our lives. One of the biggest lies we ever told in the church was, " As long as I got King Jesus, I don't need nobody else." The Bible never taught that theology. The Bible taught us that Christ would never leave nor forsake the baptized believer (Hebrews 13:5).

The extrovert with insecurities must also be conscious that people get tired too. They may have lives of their own as well. That does not mean they hate us or are trying to reject us. They may be going through personal battles that we may not know about. Have you ever had something on your mind when you walked past someone without speaking? They might have lashed out at you by saying, "You can't even say good morning." The good morning was more for them than it was for you.

The balance is knowing how to socialize but having time alone. The balance is setting time aside for ourselves just as much as we would for someone else. As they say, we all need somebody to lean on, but we all need to be alone sometimes. Christ-confident individuals feel alone, just like self-confident individuals. However, Christ-confident individuals refuse to live in their feelings; they live by faith.

I Lost My Mom and Wife at the Same Time

While I was working on this book chapter, a client, who I will call Frank, desperately sought a session with me. I didn't know why, but I agreed to meet with him. As we talked, he began to tell me how he denies having problems with alcohol. I disagreed, but I felt he wanted me to listen. That's what I kept doing. He further divulged his pain with losing his mother in the Covid-19 pandemic. Then he talked about losing his wife at the same time. It was how he lost her that interested me.

He stated, "When my mom died, my wife (who is an atheist) told me, "Forget you and your God!" This man was brought up in church and backslides. His wife, however, was a full-blown atheist who cursed her husband's God. He felt he had lost her that day. He didn't want to be alone, so he stayed and kept drinking instead of separating from her. Please don't allow anyone to separate you from the love of God (Romans 8:35-39) that is in Christ Jesus our Lord.

What's a Person Like You Doing Alone?

That's the question that King David was asked in 1 Samuel 21:1. King David was a lovable guy, but he was alone. He was on the run from his mentor. Oddly, he was traveling alone. He did not want the King to know he was scared. I feel led by God to tell you that God knows how scared you are. He is quite aware of how lonely you are. Your sister knows there is something off, your mother has been noticing the mood swings, and close friends don't even see what's wrong.

Jesus Christ wants you to know that he knows you're on the run from your past, traumas, hurts, fears, and secret sins, but call on Jesus! "Whosoever shall call on the Lord shall be saved" (Acts 2:21).

Lonely Faith

Has someone in your family slept with your man or lady? Well, that's what happened in the movie, *Soul Food.* This movie is about an African American family held together by the family's matriarch. They are called Mama Jo, played by Irma P. Hall. In this movie, Vivica A. Fox plays the middle sister, Maxine. Nia Long, the youngest, plays Bird, and Vanessa Williams plays Teri Joseph. Terri had it hard. Her sister married her ex-boyfriend (notice I did not say stole her man. People go where they want to go. Remember that before you make excuses for bad behavior).

Terri's second husband, Miles, played by Michael Beach, cheats on Teri with her cousin Faith, Gina Ravera. Now Teri was very successful, an attorney, and so was Miles. Since they had room in their house, Teri allowed Faith to stay. However, Faith used to be a stripper and upcoming video vixen who was not trusted. However, Teri does what Momma Jo would have wanted her to do.

See, Teri was unsupportive of her husband Miles' career transition, from attorney to musician. Faith came into the house and made him feel supported (emotional connection). Faith went to his concert (making time for him). Then there are the scenes where Faith and Miles talk by the fireplace (sexual tension). She explains to Miles that she is on the run. Miles, in his state of intoxication, told her a truth that she found a little hard to hear, as evidenced by her body language:

"You should stop pretending you don't need anybody because you're just lying to yourself." Faith was lonely and tried to numb it with the fast life, the bottle, and her cousin's man. I wished I could have asked lonely Faith, "Where is your faith in God"?

Things to Remember if You're Looking for a Relationship to Cure Loneliness:

- The person you want should not have to give up their alone time because you want constant me-time that you call us-time. In other words, don't use them to cure your loneliness.
- Are you looking for a partner or a personal self-esteem assistant? Do you only want this person to give constant reassurance, compliments, and attention even when they are tired and need it themselves?

- Make sure you want it but don't need it. Only Christ can support all our wants and needs. Everything you need is in Jesus.
- Are you willing to be with someone who has a mind of their own?
- They don't have to do everything you like but will do those things out of love.
- Are you sure you won't give up your life for their life?

God is the Best Provider for the Alone

When God created the world, he said everything he made was good. God, however, decided that only one thing was not good: for man to be alone (Genesis 2:18). So, God decided to support Adam. God is the best matchmaker, but we have to trust him. God cannot be manipulated into giving us someone who goes against his will for our lives. God loves us too much to let our wants kill our needs.

To be honest, some of us may never get into a relationship. Maybe we're just waiting for the right person to show up while putting our life on hold - we're hoping that the right person will eventually come, or maybe we're stuck in fear that they'll never come.

I Can't Stand Living All Alone

Singer Phyllis Hyman wrote a song called *I Can't Stand Living All Alone*. When you listen to the lyrics, it's about a woman who truly could not stand living all alone. Phyllis was beautiful to many, while she felt ugly, too tall, and unattractive. She gained over 200 pounds, had an addiction to alcohol, and was clinically diagnosed with bipolar disorder.

On June 30, 1995, she locked herself up in a room, leaving a note saying she was tired. My heart goes out to the singer who was gone too soon. However, I hope you know it's not too late to reach you. God has you reading this book for a reason. Cry out to Jesus! Phyllis told a man, but I want you to tell Jesus if you can't stand living all alone. Phyllis was trying to handle loneliness through self-confidence and committed suicide.

I pray the Holy Ghost arrests you right where you are and wraps His loving arms around you. David wrote, "This poor man cried, and the LORD heard him and saved him out of all his troubles" (Psalms 34:6).

SIX

I Don't Like What I'm Hearing

"You can only play it by ear when you've heard from God"
—Dr. Jamal H. Bryant

*W*hen people have heard what you've done, they no longer trust the positive things you are now doing. More importantly, when others have heard about what we have done, they no longer are interested in believing anything we have to say. This was the story of Paul's new life in Christ:

> *"Meanwhile, Saul was uttering threats with every breath and was eager to kill the Lord's followers.[a] So he went to the high priest. ² He requested letters addressed to the synagogues in Damascus, asking for their cooperation in arresting any followers of the Way he found there. He wanted to bring them—both men and women—back to Jerusalem in chains.³ As he was approaching Damascus on this mission, a light from heaven suddenly shone down around him. ⁴ He fell to the ground*

and heard a voice saying to him, "Saul! Saul!
Why are you persecuting me?"⁵ "Who are you,
lord?" Saul asked. And the voice replied, "I
am Jesus, the one you are persecuting! ⁶ Now
get up and go into the city, and you will be
told what you must do" (Acts 9:1-6, NLT).

Most of the New Testament scriptures are written by the apostle Paul. He would be the vessel that Jesus Christ would use to bring thousands of people to the faith. Saul used to be a killer of Christians. At that time, the baptized believers were called people of "the Way." Didn't Jesus Christ tell his disciples, "⁶ Jesus saith unto him, I am the way, the truth, and the life: no man cometh unto the Father, but by me⁷ If ye had known me, ye should have known my Father also: and from henceforth ye know him and have seen him." (John 14:6-7, KJV).

Paul believed that Christ was the God of the Old Testament, but little did he know or believe that Jesus was the Christ. We cannot be hard on Paul. He was killing and arresting Christians because he thought he was doing what God wanted him to do. Jesus even explained to his disciples, *I have told you these things so that you won't abandon your faith.* *² For you will be expelled from the synagogues, and the time is coming when those who kill you will think they are doing a holy service for God. ³ This is because they have never known the Father or me" (John 16:1-3, NLT).*

This implies that Saul persecuted the church because he did not know that Jesus was the mighty God in Christ (2 Corinthians 5:19). Paul asked the LORD to identify himself (Paul was educated enough as a monotheistic Jew, trained under Gamaliel to know that the LORD means God).

God answers him by letting him know that "I am Jesus." Unlike Peter, James, John, and the rest of the disciples who walked and talked with Jesus, Paul meets Jesus on his way to work to kill the saints, but the voice of Christ was all he needed to change the course of the rest of his life.

I Value Your Opinion

Many of us are miserable and undervalue ourselves due to the various voices we have valued over the years. Often, the voices that hurt most are the voices of people we come to love and trust. Or sometimes, they are just the people that we are stuck with. **The only danger about valuing the opinions of some is that they may not value you.**

The only danger about valuing the opinions of some is that they may not value you.

Oprah once remarked, "You can't be friends with someone who wants your life." Often, others are jealous of us; they may cater to our ego to figure us out. Remember this happened to David when Saul wanted to kill him.

> "*17 Then Saul said to David, "Here is my elder daughter Merab. I will give her to you for a wife. Only be valiant for me and fight the LORD's battles." For Saul thought, "Let not my hand be against him, but let the hand of the Philistines be against him." 18 And David said to Saul, "Who am I, and who are my relatives, my father's clan in Israel, that I should be son-in-law to the king?" 19 But when Merab, Saul's daughter, should have been given to David, she*

was given to Adriel the Meholathite for a wife.²⁰ Now Saul's daughter Michal loved David. And they told Saul, and the thing pleased him. ²¹ Saul thought, "Let me give her to him, that she may be a snare for him and that the hand of the Philistines may be against him." Therefore Saul said to David a second time,[b] "You shall now be my son-in-law." ²² And Saul commanded his servants, "Speak to David in private and say, 'Behold, the king has delight in you, and all his servants love you. Now then become the king's son-in-law.'" ²³ And Saul's servants spoke those words in the ears of David. And David said, "Does it seem to you a little thing to become the king's son-in-law since I am a poor man and have no reputation?" ²⁴ And the servants of Saul told him, "Thus and so did David speak." ²⁵ Then Saul said, "Thus shall you say to David, 'The king desires no bride-price except a hundred foreskins of the Philistines, that he may be avenged of the king's enemies.'" Now Saul thought to make David fall by the hand of the Philistines" (1 Samuel 18:17-26, ESV).

Maybe Saul was paranoid and knew David didn't trust him, so he made his men con David into believing that the King liked him. David is still wrestling with insecurities from the past that he can't see Saul for who he is. Anyone's voice can sound believable when we don't know who we are in Christ. Think the best of people without being quick to believe they always think the best of us. The Bible puts it this way:

> "⁶ *Do not eat the bread of* [a] *a selfish person; Or desire his delicacies;* ⁷ *For as he* [b] *thinks within himself, so he is. He says to you, "Eat and drink!" But his heart is not with you.* ⁸ *You will vomit up* [c] *the morsel you have eaten And waste your* [d] *compliments"* (Proverbs 23:6-8, NASB)."

Anyone's voice can sound believable when we don't know who we are in Christ. Think the best of people without being quick to believe they always think the best of us.

The Apostle Paul Didn't Have David's Problem

David had a lot of insecurities. He had an unsupportive father who appeared to think less of David. He grew up looking after sheep. He felt like his parents may forsake him, and he had past sins that he lived in guilt over. David's guilt about what he was going through only adds insult to injury. On the other hand, Paul was confident that killing Christians was the right thing to do. He was self-confident, but he had to hear the voice of the Lord Jesus to be Christ-confident.

Paul will tell you what made him appear different from King David was that he was ignorant of how he killed Christians. Paul stated,

> ¹² *And I thank Christ Jesus for our Lord who has enabled me, because He counted*

me faithful, putting me into the ministry,
13. However, I was formerly a blasphemer,
a persecutor, and an [d]insolent man. Still,
I obtained mercy because I did it igno-
rantly in unbelief. 14 And the grace of our
Lord was exceedingly abundant, with
faith and love which are in Christ Jesus. 15
This is a faithful saying and worthy of all
acceptance, that Christ Jesus came into the
world to save sinners, of whom I am chief.
16 However, for this reason, I obtained
mercy, that in me first Jesus Christ might
show all longsuffering, as a pattern to those
who will believe in Him for everlasting
life. 17 Now to the King eternal, immortal,
invisible, to [e]God who alone is wise, be
honor and glory forever and ever. Amen"
(1 Timothy 1:12-17, NKJV).

The apostle Paul did not know what he was doing before his conversion. He did not need to think he was wrong. His internal dialogue was, "I'm doing God's service by killing Christians."

Notice he acknowledged doing it ignorantly in unbelief. That means he did not believe that Jesus was God. After God changed his heart, he had a passion and gift to reach others that the original twelve disciples could not reach. The only caveat is the church does not want to listen to him because they have already heard about him, and Paul is quite aware of this!

Christ-Confident Affirmations

Low self-esteem has a lot to do with what we tell or don't tell ourselves. Our thoughts about ourselves will affect how we see ourselves. Talk to any good psychologist, and they will support that talk therapy is just as beneficial as taking medication. The good news is that most psychiatrists won't tell us that low self-esteem is treated as a symptom of depression or anxiety rather than the root because one does not need medication to fix low self-esteem. Insecurities can dissipate with a change in self-talk.

Paul spent years telling himself that he was well within his rights to persecute the Church of the Lord Jesus Christ. This is self-talk. After encountering Jesus Christ, he learns Christ-talk. Paul, who was responsible for the majority of the New Testament, makes Christ-confident affirmations. Let's look at some of them now:

- "Nay, in all these things we are more than conquerors through him that loved us" (Romans 8:3, KJV)
- "I can do all things through Christ which strengthens me" (Philippians 4:13, KJV)
- "But by the grace of God, I am what I am" (1 Corinthians 15:9)

These are just a few apostles' Christ-confident statements he gave and shared with us. It was good that he did because many of the saints at Jerusalem were not ready to hear the preacher that heard the voice of Jesus. They just could not seem to get over what he did. Question for you: Have you stopped being who Christ called you to be because of your past? Everything people have said about us is not a lie. Some of those things they have exposed or castigated us about we did.

Nevertheless, it is not what we did that they know that holds us back; it is what we say to ourselves after the mistake is over. Following Jesus Christ requires that I change the internal dialogue with myself. I no longer call myself what they called me. I no longer talk down to myself. I no longer tell myself lies to make myself feel better. I tell myself the truth about who I am. The truth begins with Jesus Christ because He is "the way, the truth, and the Life," according to John 14:6.

I Already Told on Myself

We all can tell when someone does not want us around or does not value our presence in the room. Even if they don't say anything, their body language says it all. However, those with deep-seated insecurities think everyone is against them. One of the signs that low self-worth is dominant in our lives is when we have a bad habit of reading someone's mind for them. Only that individual knows what they are thinking. However, let's say they did not want you around because they are holding your past against you.

> 1 "Brothers and fathers, hear the defense that I now make before you."
> 2 And when they heard that he was addressing them in the Hebrew language, they became even quieter. And he said:
> 3 "I am a Jew, born in Tarsus in Cilicia, but brought up in this city, educated at the feet of Gamaliel according to

the strict manner of the law of our fathers, being zealous for God as all of you are this day. 4 I persecuted this Way to the death, binding and delivering to prison both men and women, 5 as the high priest and the whole council of elders can bear me witness. I received letters from them to the brothers, and I journeyed toward Damascus to take those who were there and bring them in bonds to Jerusalem to be punished.

6 "As I was on my way and drew near to Damascus, about noon, a great light from heaven suddenly shone around me. 7 And I fell to the ground and heard a voice saying to me, 'Saul, Saul, why are you persecuting me?' 8 And I answered, 'Who are you, Lord?' And he said to me, 'I am Jesus of Nazareth, whom you are persecuting.' 9 Now, those with me saw the light but did not understand the voice of the one who was speaking to me. 10 And I said, 'What shall I do, Lord?' And the Lord said to me, 'Rise, and go into Damascus, and there you will be told all that is appointed for you to do.' 11 And since I could not see because of the brightness of that light, I was led by the hand by those who were with me and came into Damascus.

12 "And one Ananias, a devout man according to the law, well spoken of by all the Jews who lived there, 13 came to me, and standing by me said to me, 'Brother Saul, receive your sight.' And at that very hour, I

received my sight and saw him. 14 And he said, 'The God of our fathers appointed you to know his will, to see the Righteous One and to hear a voice from his mouth; 15 for you will be a witness for him to everyone of what you have seen and heard. 16 And now why do you wait? Rise and be baptized and wash away your sins, calling on his name.'

17 "When I had returned to Jerusalem and was praying in the temple, I fell into a trance 18 and saw him saying to me, 'Make haste and get out of Jerusalem quickly because they will not accept your testimony about me.' 19 And I said, 'Lord, they know that in one synagogue after another I imprisoned and beat those who believed in you. 20 And when the blood of Stephen your witness was being shed, I was standing by and approving and watching over the garments of those who killed him.' 21 And he said to me, 'Go, for I will send you far away to the Gentiles.'" (Acts 22:1-21, ESV).'"

Paul is sharing his testimony with the people. He is publicly telling the people what Christ did for him privately. When we can honestly tell ourselves the truth, we won't have a problem telling others. People cannot hurt us with a past that we have admitted the truth about to ourselves and others. Paul had no secrets; Paul had a testimony. **The devil wants us**

The devil wants us to keep our secrets to ourselves, so he can use them to talk to us in our voice.

to keep our secrets to ourselves, so he can use them to talk to us in our voice.

The church can sometimes be the hardest place to share secrets with when many already give off a condescending persona that they are above you. People go on talk shows, podcasts, instagram, facebook and expose themselves. However, there are no secrets like the ones kept in the house of the living God.

The God of My Secrets

David did not feel good knowing that he offended God. When David committed sins, it bothered him to the core. Remember in chapter one, we get a chance to see how David was overlooked, misunderstood, and the least acknowledged in his father's house. He knew how it felt to have people walk away from him because of his flaws. David held onto God because he knew God's loving kindness was better than life itself (Psalms 63:3, KJV). Therefore, David did not want to hear the only true God who healed all his wounds. Listen to what happened when David kept unconfessed sin to himself:

> *"Blessed [fortunate, prosperous, favored by God] is he whose transgression is forgiven, And whose sin is covered. Blessed is the man to whom the LORD does not impute wickedness, And in whose spirit there is no deceit. When I kept silent about my sin, my body wasted away Through my groaning all day long. For day and night, Your hand [of displeasure] was heavy upon me; My energy (vitality, strength) was drained away as*

with the burning heat of summer. Selah. I acknowledged my sin to You, And I did not hide my wickedness; I said, "I will confess [all] my transgressions to the LORD," And You forgave the guilt of my sin. Selah. Therefore, let everyone who is godly pray to You [for forgiveness] in a time when You [are near and] may be found; Surely when the great waters [of trial and distressing times] overflow, they will not reach [the spirit in] him. You are my hiding place; You, LORD, protect me from trouble; You surround me with songs and shouts of deliverance. Selah" (Psalms 32:1-7, AMP).

Notice the king acknowledged that if he kept his sins to himself, not repenting to Jesus Christ, his body felt the pains of guilt. He acknowledged the heaviness he felt due to him holding back from God. David realized that the Lord was not only his shepherd, but he was also the God of his secrets. Subsequently, David made this a habit of praying to God about his secrets. He prays, "How can I know all the sins lurking in my heart? Cleanse me from these hidden faults" (Psalms 19:12, NLT). The king found out the place to keep his secrets was the hiding place. For David, God was that hiding place (Psalms 32:7).

Maybe you grew up in a very private family and swept your rape, molestation, abandonment, daddy issues, and other family secrets under the rug to the degree to which it has affected your life in other areas. Or maybe you grew up with a family that treated you like you could do no wrong; consequently, this made it harder for you to be honest about your secrets because you're still trying to live up to an image that is doing more harm to your esteem than you realize.

Healing requires honesty. When we are honest, we may lose some people. When we tell the truth, it might cause problems in our marriage. When we are honest, it might lead to custody battles, making things better or worse. Honesty makes us better if things don't get better.

Many of us carry secret trauma that we are still experiencing nightmares, anxiety, and self-esteem attacks. I encourage you to talk to someone. Find a therapist you are comfortable with, go to your pastor, but most importantly, talk to Jesus Christ – who is our hiding place.

Self-Talk vs. Christ-Talk

Self-talk is what we say to ourselves that determines how we feel, believe, and do. We talk to ourselves all day, whether we do it out loud or internally. However, when one has chronic low self-worth, they constantly talk to themselves negatively literally all day. They tell themselves they are worthless even though they have a gift to give back to the world. They tell themselves their significant other is only with them because they have money (forgetting that their significant other was with them when they were broke). The problem with negative self-talk is that it focuses primarily on what we think is wrong with us and fabricates its own story.

Christ-talk is when we say to ourselves what Christ says about us. That means if Christ says I am His child, that's what I say to myself even when I don't feel like I'm His child. The best way to change how we feel about ourselves in Christ is to watch what we say to ourselves. The one whose confidence is in the Lord Jesus knows how to talk themselves

The best thing to tell yourself is what Christ told you about you through his word and by His Holy Spirit.

through moments of anxiety, reminding themselves how much Christ loves them. The Christ-confident individual does not speak self-affirmations; the Christ-confident individuals speak Christ-affirmations. **The best thing to tell yourself is what Christ told you about you through his word and by His Holy Spirit.**

Say it Loud

"Say It Loud" was an African American colloquialism that started back in August 1968 from a James Brown song. Brown wanted African Americans to be comfortable in their skin. However, low self-worth is not a color thing. It's a human thing. One of the biggest signs of insecurity is not speaking up for oneself or not speaking loud enough.

Many have insecurities that stem from their opinions not being valued growing up. Maybe your parents saw you as unintelligent because you didn't go to college. Many adults who have high corporate jobs have become successful attorneys, even public speakers, still have a hard time speaking up for themselves to certain family members or those close to them. It's a fight to walk in courage when we have no confidence to face who we need to face.

> *"46-48 They spent some time in Jericho. As Jesus was leaving town, trailed by his disciples and a parade of people, a blind beggar by the name of Bartimaeus, son of Timaeus, was sit-*

ting alongside the road. When he heard that Jesus the Nazarene was passing by, he began to cry out, "Son of David, Jesus! Mercy, have mercy on me!" Many tried to hush him up, but he yelled all the louder, "Son of David! Mercy, have mercy on me!"⁴⁹⁻⁵⁰ Jesus stopped in his tracks. "Call him over." They called him. "It's your lucky day! Get up! He's calling you to come!" Throwing off his coat, he was on his feet at once and came to Jesus.⁵¹ Jesus said, "What can I do for you? The blind man said, "Rabbi, I want to see."⁵² "On your way," said Jesus. "Your faith has saved and healed you." In that very instant, he recovered his sight and followed Jesus down the road" (Mark 10:46-52, MSG).

Bartimaeus might have been blind, but he would not be quiet. He heard Jesus was passing by, and he was not afraid to ask for what he wanted. The holy scriptures assure us that they that call on the name of Jesus will be saved (Acts 2:21). Maybe they thought his self-worth was so low that they could shut him up. Not so. He refused to be quiet. Many people who struggle with low self-esteem have childhood wounds from loved ones who persuaded them to keep quiet. So even as an adult, they watch what they say in the boardroom, in a business meeting, refuse to speak up for themselves in their relationships, and say what they want even when they are made aware of their privileges and rights. Not another day, I say! Not another day in Jesus's name.

Many of us are afraid to lose people who have helped us in the past if we speak up. Bartimaeus has been blind for so long, begging for so long, and being assisted for so long that maybe losing them crossed his mind. The good news, nevertheless, was that Jesus crossed his path, and he was not about to be denied. He was not waiting for someone to speak to Jesus for him. He spoke up for himself.

Notice in the above passage that Jesus stood still when Bartimaeus kept asking Jesus for mercy. Don't allow the insecurities that your family gave you to keep you silent. Just because your family tuned you out doesn't mean Jesus can't hear you. Just because friends tuned you out, refusing to listen, doesn't mean that Jesus can't hear you. When you call on Jesus, he stops what he does for you. Many of us may not need a miracle right now; we just want to be heard. Christ hears your humble cry.

Why Don't You Want Me to Say Anything?

It is not just the child molester who gives candy to the child to keep them quiet. It's not just the one being blackmailed by the individual who gets hush money. The husband doesn't want to hear about you fulfilling your dreams of going back to school. It is also that loyal friend of yours who gets tired of hearing you talk about being independent. What do you do when you love those who don't want you to have a voice?

It is dangerous to be around people who do not want you to think for yourself, have your own mind, and live in the shadows of their insecurities. If you stay in the box they built for you, move when they move, speak when they speak to you, then they promise they will love you. Meanwhile, your hopes, dreams, and what Christ put in your spirit is on life support. They don't want you to say anything about your future because they are still living in the self-doubt of their past. That kind of circle is not healthy for you even if they love you. We can't fight the good fight of faith and fight pettiness simultaneously.

Losing My Voice

Not everyone loses their voice when they have sung too much, yelled too much, or talked too much. Many of us lose our voices in trauma. Abuse will make you lose your voice. Betrayal will make you hold everything in. Emotional abuse will make you lose your voice after being paralyzed by the anxieties and fears from yesterday's hell. We will never gain Christ-confidence if we don't take something for all that silence. Don't worry. You're in good company. Mephibosheth knows how you feel.

> *"4 Jonathan, the son of Saul, had a son who was crippled in his feet. He was five years old when the news about Saul and Jonathan came from Jezreel, and his nurse took him up and fled, and as she fled in her haste, he fell and became lame. And his name was Mephibosheth" (2 Samuel 4:4, ESV)*

Mephibosheth was only five years old. A time of innocence for him. He did not do anything wrong in the above scene. He just got caught in the commotion of adults who were at one another's throats. The nurse was doing the best she could, and all she knew was to save him. She did her best, and it cost the five-year-old his feet. This affected him into his adulthood. Just listen to how he talks about himself:

> *"And David said, "Is there still anyone left of the house of Saul, that I may show him kindness for Jonathan's sake?" 2 Now there was a servant of the house of Saul whose name was Ziba, and they called him to*

David. And the king said to him, "Are you Ziba?" And he said, "I am your servant." ³ And the king said, "Is there not still someone of the house of Saul, that I may show the kindness of God to him?" Ziba said to the king, "There is still a son of Jonathan; he is crippled in his feet." ⁴ The king said to him, "Where is he?" And Ziba said to the king, "He is in the house of Machir, the son of Ammiel, at Lo-debar." ⁵ Then King David sent and brought him from the house of Machir, the son of Ammiel, at Lo-debar. ⁶ And Mephibosheth the son of Jonathan, son of Saul, came to David and fell on his face and paid homage. And David said, "Mephibosheth!" And he answered, "Behold, I am your servant." ⁷ And David said to him, "Do not fear, for I will show you kindness for the sake of your father Jonathan, and I will restore to you all the land of Saul, your father, and you shall eat at my table always." ⁸ And he paid homage and said, "What is your servant, that you should show regard for a dead dog such as I?" (2 Samuel 9:1-8, ESV).

Notice in Verse 8 that Mephibosheth called himself "a dead dog." He is not crippled, but he depended on others for a commute, and as a man, he felt emasculated. He was disabled for life. What's worse than crippled feet is a crippled tongue. He called himself a "dead dog" because he could no longer walk.

Have you been secretly calling yourself fat, ugly, undesirable, or limiting yourself due to your age? God wanted to use King David to bring Mephibosheth to a place of honor. His crippled feet were not the handicap; his mouth was his handicap. The biggest roadblock to our destination is not the trauma. Some women (and men) have been raped and survived to tell the story. Some men have been molested and use their stories to help thousands of brothers suffering in silence.

A Christ-Confident Commitment

I want you to pause right now and make a commitment to yourself that you are no longer going to call yourself out of your name. You will no longer base your identity on the trauma you have been through. Commit to only calling yourself what Christ calls you. Just in case you need help with this. Here are some scriptures about what Jesus Christ wants us to know about our identity in him:

> *"But you are not like that, for you are a chosen people. You are royal priests, a holy nation, God's very own possession. As a result, you can show others the goodness of God, for he called you out of the darkness into his wonderful light." -1 Peter 2:9, NLT*

> *"Yet in all these things we are more than conquerors through Him who loved us." -Romans 8:37, NKJV*

> *"The LORD appeared to him from far away. I have loved you with an everlasting love;*

therefore, I have continued my faithfulness to you." -Jeremiah 31:3, ESV

"We love because he first loved us." -1 John 4:19, ESV

"For the mountains may depart and the hills are removed, but my steadfast love shall not depart from you, and my covenant of peace shall not be removed," says the LORD, who has compassion on you." -Isaiah 54:10, ESV

"Anyone who does not love does not know God because God is love." -1 John 4:8, ESV

"The Joy of the LORD is your strength." -Nehemiah 8:10

Go Where Your Words Matter

"[a]Brothers and fathers, hear my defense which I now offer to you."
² And when they heard that he was addressing them in the [b]Hebrew dialect, they became even quieter. He *said, ³ "I am a Jew, born in Tarsus of Cilicia, but brought up in this city, educated [c]under Gamaliel, [d]strictly according to the Law of our fathers, being zealous for God just as you all are today. ⁴ I persecuted this Way to the death, binding and putting both men

and women into prisons, [5] as also the high priest and all the Council of the elders [e] can testify. From them, I also received letters from the brothers. I started for Damascus to bring even those there to Jerusalem [f] as prisoners to be punished.

[6] "But it happened that as I was on my way, approaching Damascus at about noon, a very bright light suddenly flashed from heaven all around me, [7] and I fell to the ground and heard a voice saying to me, 'Saul, Saul, why are you persecuting Me?' [8] And I answered, 'Who are You, Lord?' And He said to me, 'I am Jesus the Nazarene, whom you are persecuting.' [9] And those with me saw the light but did not [g] understand the voice of the One who was speaking to me. [10] And I said, 'What shall I do, Lord?' And the Lord said to me, 'Get up and go on into Damascus, and there you will be told about everything that has been appointed for you to do.' [11] But since I could not see because of the [h] brightness of that light, I came into Damascus being led by the hand by those who were with me.

[12] "Now a certain Ananias, a man who was devout by the standard of the Law and well spoken of by all the Jews who lived there, [13] came to me, and standing nearby he said to me, 'Brother Saul, receive your sight!' And [i] at that very moment I looked up at him. [14] And he said, 'The God of our fathers has appointed you to know His will

*and to see the Righteous One and to hear a
[i]message from His mouth. 15 For you will be
a witness for Him to all people of what you
have seen and heard. 16 Now, why do you
delay? Get up and be baptized and wash
away your sins by calling on His name.'*

*17 "It happened when I returned to
Jerusalem and was praying in the temple, that I fell into a trance, 18 and I saw
Him saying to me, 'Hurry and get out of
Jerusalem quickly because they will not
accept your testimony about Me.' 19 And
I said, 'Lord, they understand that in one
synagogue after another I used to imprison
and beat those who believed in You. 20 And
when the blood of Your witness Stephen was
being shed, I also was standing nearby and
approving, and watching over the cloaks of
those who were killing him.' 21 And He said
to me, 'Go! For I will send you far away to
the Gentiles" (Acts 22:1-21, NASB).*

In our human psychology, we tend to focus on those
who don't celebrate, validate, or support us. It plays with our
minds and leaves us in limbo, questioning our Christ-given
capabilities. We can have a hundred people celebrate, but we
are still focused on the two who did not. Until we develop
the Christ-confidence (that does not happen overnight, especially when we didn't always have it), we will continually
chase those who left us, leave early, or aren't coming back.

Paul is a changed man. In the above passage, he shares
his story on how Jesus changed his life. He is excited to
preach the good news about Jesus Christ. However, he is

quite mindful that everyone is unhappy because they remember who he used to be. To critical church folk, he wasn't just a sinner. He was evil. He was a killer, and God could not have changed someone like Paul. What that is saying is the people of Jerusalem do not believe in the power of Jesus Christ to forgive sins.

Sadly, there will be many in the church that may hold on to your mistakes, but do like my grandma said, "Hold to God's unchanging hands." It's challenging to walk through a crowd that body language demonstrates, "You got some nerve bringing your sinful self in here. God is not thinking about you." That's their prerogative. Be who Jesus Christ called you to be instead of holding your past against you. No devil in hell and no grudge holder on earth can unforgive who Jesus Christ has already forgiven; I mean no devil, no grudge holder. I don't care how good their memory is.

Jesus Christ knew that many Jews would not believe Paul was changed. That is why Jesus told him, "And He said to me, 'Go! For I will send you far away to the Gentiles'" (Acts 22:21, NASB). What Christ has done in Paul's life would not be altered or eradicated by anyone in his past, present, or future.

Self-Confidence vs. Christ-Confidence

A self-confident individual is focused on proving a point to those who hurt them. A self-confident individual wants the people who threw dirt on them to see they made it. A self-confident individual may post their new car on facebook because they want other people to see their wins. A self-confident individual is focused on getting the attention of those who they no longer need.

On the other hand, the Christ-confident mindset is not praying to be blessed to rub it in their enemy's face. The Christ-confident individual knows that if it had not been for the LORD on their side, they would have lost their mind a long time ago. A Christ-confident individual is no longer preoccupied with who is not there. Their focus is on Jesus, the author, and finisher of their faith (Hebrews 12:2, KJV). A Christ-confident individual will not take their anger out on those who stayed over the people who left. The Christ confident individual is just excited to be free in Jesus Christ.

Give You to Who Receives You

Often, we hear the voices in our head always reminding us of who rejected us, abandoned us, left us, and is no longer there for us. Many of us have been chasing people who won't return. We are checking their social media because it's been a few weeks, and they have not accepted our apology nor called us back. Jesus Christ does not want us living that way. We can only ask someone to forgive us; we cannot make them.

Please make up your mind that you will not continue to chase people who don't want to be bothered. As Bishop T. D. Jakes of *the Potter's House Church* stated:

"When people can walk away from you, let them walk. I don't want you to spend another day trying to talk somebody into loving you, calling you, caring about you, coming by to see you. I mean, hang up the phone because your destiny is not tied to the person who left. If they walked away, it's no accident. People leave you because they are not joined to you. The Bible said, 'They went out from us, but they were not of us; for if they had been of us, they would no doubt have continued with us" (1 John 2:19, KJV). Accept it as the will of God when you tried to make it work, and it didn't work. Wash your face and let them go!"

Go where you are accepted. I don't care if it is one person. We wish everyone would love and let things go in a perfect world, but that does not always happen. Hold your head up and stop wasting time with the people who love you talking about the ones who don't.

How Did Jesus Handle Rejection?

The Bible says that Jesus Christ was despised and rejected, a man of sorrows, acquainted with grief (Isaiah 53:3, NLT). Jesus knows what it was like to be rejected. He was rejected to the degree of being spit on, lied to, beaten, whipped, and nailed to a wooden cross. Jesus Christ was rejected for you. He was rejected for the rejects. He didn't take all that rejection for you to talk to yourself like a reject. So, let's see how Christ wants us to respond to rejection:

> "[10] He was in the world, and the world came into being through Him, and yet the world did not [j]know Him. [11] He came to His [k]own, and His people did not [l]accept Him. [12] But [m]as many as received Him, to them He gave the right to become children of God, to those who [n]believe in His name," (John 1:10-12, NASB).

Jesus Christ shows us that the best way to deal with rejection is to give ourselves to those that will receive us. Jesus Christ will always have someone that will receive you. He will give you people who want to collaborate with you. He will send the right connections. We have to focus on who is acceptinging of us as we walk in Christ's confidence.

When You're No Longer the Flavor of the Month

> *"⁴ Finally, all the elders of Israel met at Ramah to discuss the matter with Samuel. ⁵ "Look," they told him, "you are now old, and your sons are not like you. Give us a king to judge us as all the other nations have."⁶ Samuel was displeased with their request and went to the LORD for guidance. ⁷ "Do everything they say to you," the LORD replied, "for they are rejecting me, not you. They don't want me to be their king any longer. ⁸ Ever since I brought them from Egypt, they have continually abandoned me and followed other gods. And now they are giving you the same treatment. ⁹ Do as they ask, but solemnly warn them about the way a king will reign over them" (1 Samuel 8:4-9, NLT).*

We are a modern culture. We like what's trending. We like the latest style. We are constantly taking ideas from others to appear to look the smartest, best, most beautiful, and the most popular. Insecurity is never satisfied with a Christ-given identity. When we are insecure, we tell ourselves how others view us as more harmful than good. Insecurity will have us in a place of unhealthy comparisons.

Samuel was the prophet of his day. He would put all of today's prophets to shame. Samuel was respected when he walked down the street. He was God's prophet till death, but he was respected by the people as long as he was young. People love you when you're young and able. Samuel was the flavor of the month until he grew older and became less palatable.

When he got old, they told him they wanted to replace him because he was too old. Can you imagine how hurt the prophet was? He did not do anything to them. They enjoyed him, but they wanted to be like other nations. God had to intervene and tell the prophet that they didn't just reject him, but God as well.

What if you saw your rejection that way? What if you told yourself, "They didn't reject me; they rejected a child of the highest God." Change how you talk to yourself about rejection.

End the Comparisons

There are two ways that many with low self-esteem independently handle their insecurities. The first is through arrogance. Arrogance is not confidence. Read that twice. I have met some arrogant individuals who thought they were covering up their insecurities, but they showed more. We will always act like the person we think we are. The arrogant individual with low self-esteem often must be the loudest in the room. If they are not acknowledged, they don't come around anymore.

In some cases, if you don't speak to them first, they block you off social media. They can appear to be a cocky know-it-all who is full of themselves and very argumentative. This is the kind of low self-worth that dims the lights of others to make themselves look good. Here are other ways insecure individuals come off as arrogant:

- Overly boastful
- Highlighting what talents they have and others don't

- Always talking about themselves
- Treating others like they are less than
- Ignoring the feeling of others
- Telling others how they're better than them.
- Being controlling

Secondly, the other way people handle their insecurities is through feelings of inferiority. They constantly berate themselves when given compliments. They downplay their accomplishments, focus on their failures, and discuss who left them. Here is a list of other ways many with low self-esteem come off inferior to others:

- Avoiding what they want to do out of fear of rejection, castigation, or failing
- Thinking others have better ideas than them
- Throwing their dreams away because they deem them too small or unachievable
- Focusing on what they cannot do
- Staying quiet when they know the answer
- Unable to set boundaries
- Unable to accept love and help from others
- Not wanting to seek therapy, sponsor, or preacher advice
- Denying wants and needs to satisfy everyone else

A wise woman once said, "Comparing ourselves is comparing our worst to somebody's best." Many with low self-esteem use comparing to rate themselves. You cannot use someone else to guide what God will do in your life. The best thing we can do for ourselves is to compare who we think we are with who Jesus Christ wants us to be. As the gospel singer Albertina Walker used to sing, "I'm yours LORD. Everything I am, everything I'm not, and everything I've got." Don't spend the rest of your life focusing on what you don't have or who you don't have. God has given us all that's needed for life and godliness (2 Peter 1:3, KJV).

You Talk Too Much

Many of us have that one friend we know we can't share things with. We love that friend that wants the best for others, knowing that they mean well. However, as the saying goes: Loose lips sink ships. I am referring to talking too much about what went wrong in our past, talking like a victim, talking like there is nothing good about us. Many of us are right on the verge of what Jesus Christ wants to do in our lives. Still, we are so quick to talk down to ourselves to the degree to which we forget that Christ can bless us in the face of our thoughts and feelings of low self-worth.

> "Moses objected, "They won't trust me. They won't listen to a word I say. They're going to say, 'GOD? Appear to him? Hardly!'"
>
> ² So GOD said, "What's that in your hand?"
>
> "A staff."
>
> ³ "Throw it on the ground." He threw it. It became a snake; Moses jumped back—fast!
>
> ⁴⁻⁵ GOD said to Moses, "Reach out and grab it by the tail." He reached out and grabbed it—and he was holding his staff again. "That's so they will trust that GOD appeared to you, the God of their fathers, the God of Abraham, the God of Isaac, and the God of Jacob."

⁶ GOD then said, "Put your hand inside your shirt." He slipped his hand under his shirt, then took it out. His hand had turned leprous, like snow.

⁷ He said, "Put your hand back under your shirt." He did it, then took it back out—as healthy as before.

⁸⁻⁹ "So if they don't trust you and aren't convinced by the first sign, the second sign should do it. But if it doesn't, if even after these two signs they don't trust you and listen to your message, take some water out of the Nile and pour it out on the dry land; the Nile water that you pour out will turn to blood when it hits the ground."

¹⁰ Moses raised another objection to GOD: "Master, please, I don't talk well. I've never been good with words, neither before nor after you spoke to me. I stutter and stammer."

¹¹⁻¹² GOD said, "And who do you think made the human mouth? And who makes some mute, some deaf, some sighted, some blind? Isn't it I, GOD? So, get going. I'll be right there with you—with your mouth! I'll be right there to teach you what to say."

¹³ He said, "Oh, Master, please! Send somebody else" (Exodus 4:1-13, MSG).

Moses comes off as a drama queen. Do you hear the anxiety in his voice? Do you see how he was about to talk himself out of what Jesus Christ called him to do because he was self-conscious instead of Christ-conscious? That's not just Moses. Many of us internally talk like that when Christ speaks to us about greatness. We are so focused on what we cannot do that we fail to walk in obedience to the call of Christ in our lives. There is a direct correlation between disobedience and low self-worth. God had one question for the soon-to-be leader's feelings of inferiority: "[11-12] GOD said, "And who do you think made the human mouth? And who makes some mute, some deaf, some sighted, some blind? Isn't it I, GOD?" (Exodus 4:11-12, MSG)

Do you see how much therapy the scriptures have for our insecurities? The next time you think about how you're not as good as someone else, ask yourself: Who made you? The next time your mother compares you to your sister, ask: Who made you? The next time you focus on who took your man, ask yourself: Who made you? The next time you think about getting cosmetic surgery, ask yourself: Who made you? Baby, God makes no junk! You belong to Jesus Christ. Remember to tell yourself who God is when you don't know who you are! Our Jesus is a great God.

Voices in the Night

The apostle Paul did not allow anyone to stop him from what Christ called him to do. He was passionate, on fire, and charged up. Then the enemies wanted to kill him. But during all the commotion, God gave him a word in the night. Nighttime is tricky. Nighttime will make you call people you would not normally call during the day. Nighttime is where insecure people over-analyze their day, berating themselves for things they said or did or things they failed not to say or do.

> *[11] That night, the Lord appeared to Paul and said, "Be encouraged, Paul. Just as you*

have been a witness to me here in Jerusalem,
you must preach the Good News in Rome as
well" (Acts 23:11, NLT).

Listen, when you can't sleep, be careful what you tell yourself. When you're not happy with how you look, feel, or behave, watch what you tell yourself. Now is a good time to ask if you are filled with the Holy Spirit. Do you speak in tongues as the spirit of God gives you the ability? The only way to build ourselves up, at the end or the start of the day, is to pray in the spirit.

I need the Holy Ghost to speak through me when I'm getting ready to speak negatively or verbalize thoughts of doubt.

> *"26 And the Holy Spirit helps us in our weakness. For example, we don't know what God wants us to pray for. But the Holy Spirit prays for us with groanings that cannot be expressed in words" (Romans 8:26, NLT).*

Why Didn't You Speak Up for Me

> *"36 One of the Pharisees asked Jesus to have dinner with him, so Jesus went to his home and sat down to eat.[h] 37 When a certain immoral woman from that city heard he was eating there, she brought a beautiful alabaster jar filled with expensive perfume. 38 Then she knelt behind him at his feet, weeping. Her tears fell on his feet, and she wiped them off with her hair. Then she kept kissing his feet and putting perfume on them.*

³⁹ *When the Pharisee who had invited him saw this, he said to himself, "If this man were a prophet, he would know what kind of woman is touching him. She's a sinner!"*

⁴⁰ *Then Jesus answered his thoughts. "Simon," he said to the Pharisee, "I have something to say to you."*

"Go ahead, Teacher," Simon replied.

⁴¹ *Then Jesus told him this story: "A man loaned money to two people—500 pieces of silver^[i] to one and 50 pieces to the other. ⁴² But neither of them could repay him, so he kindly forgave them both, canceling their debts. Who do you suppose loved him more after that?"*

⁴³ *Simon answered, "I suppose the one for whom he canceled the larger debt."*

"That's right," Jesus said. ⁴⁴ Then he turned to the woman and said to Simon, "Look at this woman kneeling here. When I entered your home, you didn't offer me water to wash the dust from my feet, but she has washed them with her tears and wiped them with her hair. ⁴⁵ You didn't greet me with a kiss, but from the time I first came in, she has not stopped kissing my feet. ⁴⁶ You neglected the courtesy of olive oil to anoint my head, but she has anointed my feet with rare perfume.

⁴⁷ *"I tell you, her sins—and they are many—have been forgiven, so she has shown me much love. But a person who is forgiven little shows only a little love." ⁴⁸ Then Jesus said to the woman, "Your sins are forgiven."*

⁴⁹ The men at the table said among themselves, "Who is this man that he goes around forgiving sins?"

⁵⁰ And Jesus said to the woman, "Your faith has saved you; go in peace" (Luke 7:36-49, NLT).

Many of us have hidden, and unresolved anger against those we feel have not spoken up for us in the past. We feel as if they did not have our backs. It has been said that the child who has been molested never forgets the parent that did it. However, they don't forgive the other parent who does not believe them. This anonymous woman came in to see Jesus, but they had something to say. They never said it out loud, but Jesus picked up on her thoughts. Jesus was God in the flesh.

God knows you are hurt because they did not speak up for you, defend you, or have your back. There are no excuses, but I want you to know that Jesus Christ will speak up for you. God may not speak when you want him, but when he speaks, Jesus is right on time!

Speak for Yourself

¹⁸ The Jewish leaders refused to believe the man had been blind and could now see, so they called in his parents. ¹⁹ They asked them, "Is this your son? Was he born blind? If so, how can he now see?"

²⁰ His parents replied, "We know this is our son and that he was born blind, ²¹, but we don't know how he can see or who healed him. Ask him. He is old enough to speak for himself." ²² His parents said this because they were afraid of the Jewish leaders. The latter had announced that anyone saying Jesus was the Messiah would be expelled from the synagogue. ²³ That's why they said, "He is old enough. Ask him."

²⁴ So for the second time, they called in the man who had been blind and told him, "God should get the glory for this,[b] because we know this man Jesus is a sinner."

²⁵ "I don't know whether he is a sinner," the man replied. "But I know this: I was blind, and now I can see!"

²⁶ "But what did he do?" they asked. "How did he heal you?"

²⁷ "Look!" the man exclaimed. "I told you once. Didn't you listen? Why do you want to hear it again? Do you want to become his disciples, too?"

²⁸ Then they cursed him and said, "You are his disciple, but we are disciples of Moses! ²⁹ We know God spoke to Moses, but we don't even know where this man comes from."

³⁰ "Why, that's very strange!" the man replied. "He healed my eyes, and yet you don't know where he comes from? ³¹ We know that God doesn't listen to sinners, but he is ready to hear those who worship him and do his will. ³² Ever since the world began, no one has been able to open the eyes of someone born blind. ³³ If this man were not from God, he couldn't have done it."

³⁴ "You were born a total sinner!" they answered. "Are you trying to teach us?" And they threw him out of the synagogue" (John 9:18-34, NLT).

Jesus healed a blind man. Jesus gave him sight. And the Pharisees had a problem. They did not believe Jesus was God in the flesh. They asked the man's parents to attest to their son's sight. I read the above passage years ago and thought these parents were cruel. However, in all actuality, they were just scared. They did not want to be put out of the synagogue. Maybe your mother did not speak up for you because she did not want to lose her boyfriend or husband. Maybe your friends did not speak up for you because they didn't want to be pushed out of the clique. Fear will make loyal individuals look like Judas.

Could it be possible God allowed them not to speak for you so that you can learn to speak for yourself? We will never reach the apex where Christ would have us go until we speak for ourselves. Consequently, when the blind man, who Jesus healed, spoke for himself, they threw him out of the synagogue. So what? At least he stood up for himself. I pray you make up your mind to talk in Christ-confidence, speaking for yourself even if your friends give you an eviction notice.

Speak Christ-Like to Yourself

¹ As the deer longs for streams of water,
So I long for you, O God.
² I thirst for God, the living God.
When can I go and stand before him?
³ Day and night I have only tears for food,

while my enemies continually taunt me, saying,
"Where is this God of yours?"
⁴ My heart is breaking as I remember how it used to be:
I walked among the crowds of worshipers,
leading a great procession to the house of God,
Singing for joy and giving thanks amid
the sound of a great celebration!
⁵ Why am I discouraged?
Why is my heart so sad?
I will put my hope in God!
I will praise him again—
My Savior and ⁶ my God!
Now I am deeply discouraged,
but I will remember you—
even from distant Mount Hermon, the source of the Jordan,
From the land of Mount Mizar.
⁷ I hear the tumult of the raging seas
As your waves and surging tides sweep over me.
⁸ But each day the LORD pours his unfailing love upon me,
and through each night I sing his songs,
Praying to God who gives me life.
⁹ "O God, my rock," I cry,
"Why have you forgotten me?
Why must I wander around in grief,
oppressed by my enemies?"
¹⁰ Their taunts break my bones.
They scoff, "Where is this God of yours?"
¹¹ Why am I discouraged?
Why is my heart so sad?
I will put my hope in God!
I will praise him again—my Savior and my God!

The writer of Psalms 42 had no therapist. There was no suicide hotline to call or crisis intervention network. Nevertheless, he talked himself through it. As someone who works in the counseling field, trust me when I tell you most experts agree that talk therapy is very beneficial for those with severe trauma and wounds from the past. Psychiatrists prescribe medication to a multitude of diagnoses across the mental health spectrum, but my specialty is showing you your worth. Other experts in self-esteem will tell you that you don't need medication for low self-esteem. It is a one-day-at-a-time type of journey.

However, I am a Christian counselor, so I believe in prayer, praying in tongues, walking in the joy of the LORD effectively. I also believe that talking and singing to ourselves is a very therapeutic intervention for those who want to be Christ-confident.

> "*18 Don't be drunk with wine because that will ruin your life. Instead, be filled with the Holy Spirit, 19 singing psalms and hymns and spiritual songs among yourselves, and making music to the Lord in your hearts*" (Ephesians 5:18-19, NLT).

Without a therapist, group therapy, or psychotherapy, the church knew the importance of singing and speaking the right words to ourselves. One of my all-time favorite scriptures on confidence is Hebrews 10:35-39:

> "*35 Cast not away, therefore, your confidence, which hath great recompense of reward.*
> *36 For ye need patience, that, after ye have done the will of God, ye might receive the promise.*

37 For yet a little while, and he that shall come will come, and will not tarry.

38 Now the just shall live by faith: but if any man draws back, my soul shall have no pleasure in him.

39 But we are not of them who draw back unto perdition; but of them, that believe to the saving of the soul."

Interestingly, the Greek word for confidence in this text is the word *parrhesia*, which comes from "pan," meaning: "all," and "*herma*," which means: "speech." So, it means: "all speech." Its dominant idea is boldness and confidence, which are exhibited in freedom of speech. Confidence, at its core, begins with looking at what we say to ourselves. If it's in our mouths, it's in our future!

CHAPTER
SEVEN

I Keep Finding the Right Kind of Love in the Wrong Place

"How did you get here? Nobody's supposed to be here. I tried that love thing for the last time."
—Deborah Cox

"You got me," was the small gentle whisper of Jesus to me one night a few years ago after a friend walked away unexpectedly. Now you may say, "Preacher, didn't you know that already?" Of course! However, having a relationship with God does not always mean we value or prioritize it. The moment we begin to put others on a pedestal like Christ himself, it's idolatry and a downfall waiting to happen. Only worship God! I repeat, only worship the Lord Jesus Christ, the Almighty!

Searching for love around us instead of above us always keeps a cycle of insecurity going within us. If we don't trade our self-confidence for Christ-confidence, we will die an early death looking for the wrong people to give us the right feeling.

Many of us cannot be content with what we have because we focus on what we don't have. This is the core conflict of the relentless pursuit of validation. Searching for love around us instead of above us always keeps a cycle of insecurity going within us. **If we don't trade our self-confidence for Christ-confidence, we will die an early death looking for the wrong people to give us the right feeling.**

Sexual Healing

I often tell my clients in addiction counseling, "There can be no self-control where there is no self-esteem. Where there is no self-esteem, we self-destruct. When we self-destruct, we self-medicate." One of the saddest cases I've heard was concerning the life of R&B soul singer Marvin Gaye. He was the son of a preacher. His father was a cross-dresser who sent images of confusion throughout Gaye's childhood. Marvin Gaye's mother stated ongoing jealousy and hatred that "my husband had for Marvin since he came out of the womb."

Even after Marvin Gaye had succeeded, reaching the top of the billboard charts, his father refused to acknowledge or speak words of affirmation into his son's life. Yes, success does not take away the human desire to hear our parents say they are proud of us. Consequently, Gaye began to experiment with cocaine, the wrong crowd, lost so much hope, and eventually moved in with his parents again.

For most of Marvin's life, he felt that he could not win. On April 1, 1984, he was shot twice by his father. Just two years before his death, he wrote about needing sexual healing. Those were not just lyrics; that's precisely what he was doing. He had married a woman as half as young as he was, mixing sex and drugs all without his father's love. It is not just the kid whose father left that's hurting; Marvin is hurting over a father who never showed up emotionally.

In my line of work, I have had the opportunity to work with clients who were abandoned by their parents, tossed in foster care, bouncing from house to house, and left with no sense of love and belonging. Others have grown up in chaotic families with verbal, emotional, and physical abuse. However, not everyone in addiction came from a broken home. Some kids had it all. Let's go to work. Grab your Bible. Turn to Luke chapter 15.

> *"11 Then He said, "A certain man had two sons. 12 The younger of them [inappropriately] said to his father, 'Father, give me the share of the property that falls to me.' So he divided the estate between them. 13 A few days later, the younger son gathered everything [that he had] and traveled to a distant country. There he wasted his fortune in reckless and immoral living. 14 Now, when he had spent everything, a severe famine occurred in that country, and he began to do without and be in need. 15 So he went and forced himself on one of the citizens of that country, who sent him into his fields to [a]feed pigs. 16 He would have gladly eaten the [carob] pods that the pigs were eating [but they could not satisfy his hunger], and no one was giving anything to him" (AMP).*

Many referred to this as the "prodigal son" story. However, if we examine this story closely, it is more about the father's love than the son's mistakes. This boy had it all. What do you give a child that has it all? Sometimes the question is, what do you give a child that wants freedom without identity? This younger son knew who his father was, knew what his father had in store for him, knew that it was the Jewish custom to wait till his father died to get his portion of the inheritance. Still, the urgency of now feeds his insecurities. He did not know who he was. The door opens to sin when we are locked out of the identity of who we are in Jesus Christ.

He felt insecure without the power to control his stuff. When we are insecure, we cannot wait for later, so we need more freedom, control, power, reassurance, love, and affection to feel better about ourselves now. Or, one may believe without the latest name brand, designer shoe, or using their Amazon Prime membership, they won't feel good about themselves. The son getting his share of his father's estate now would not make him any richer than he already was. He was born into money, but he wanted it in his hand.

More dangerous than the relentless pursuit of validation, it has us placing what should only be in God's hand into the hands of others whose validation we so desperately seek. The enemy pulls the same trick on those with low self-esteem, like Eve in the garden and the son in this story. First, the son makes us question the father's word, timing, and control, which leads to the next thing: self-doubt and being overly self-conscious. There are a few pointers that we can get from this story. Are you ready?

- **He didn't want more love; he wanted freedom.**

    He didn't do well with rules. Many of us don't like rules because we were raised in houses (not homes) where rules made us question love. Some had parents who gave them rules and an STD from sexually abusing them. Some were beaten by their father until they only thought insecure thoughts about themselves. Studies show that most incarcerated men had a problem with authority growing up. What hurts more is when we are assaulted, abused (verbally, emotionally, sexually, or physically), we become too afraid to stand up or speak for ourselves.

Consequently, we become skeptical around innocent people. As a result, we lower our expectations of people, not just in authority, but even the ones who have come to help us. This is no coincidence at all. Satan wants us to say we love God without obeying Christ. Jesus Christ once asked, "So why do you keep calling me 'Lord, Lord!' when you don't do what I say" (Luke 6:46, NLT).

The enemy used authority figures who abused their authority to traumatize us so that we won't accept the commandments of Christ. If you notice, many religious arguments are over whether the church has too many rules. What we call rules are Christ's boundaries.

Jesus reminded the church that "if you love me, obey my commandments" (John 14:15). Because Jesus loves us, he refuses to let us walk all over him. If you want to be Christ-confident like Jesus, refuse to let people mistreat you in the name of love. Boundaries must be set to confirm that you love yourself in a Christ-like way.

- **Moving further away from God won't bring us closer to finding the love we want.**
 Are you secretly mad at God, can't stand the church, or think faith in Christ is a waste of your time? I never will forget preaching a sermon years

ago on being angry with God. I asked the congregation to raise their hands if they got mad with God. A preacher on the side of me angrily blurted out, "I ain't never got mad with the LORD." The problem with the church is that we are so holy that we forget to be honest. Mary and Martha got mad at Jesus for letting their brother Lazarus die (John, Chapter 11). Jeremiah got mad at God for blessing the wicked and letting them just suffer (Jeremiah, Chapter 12). And let's not forget Jonah got so mad at God, and he tried to run from the presence of God (Jonah, Chapters 1-4). Many of us have learned the hard way that God is love. Before we look for love from someone else, we must ensure it is secured in him.

- **We waste our substance when we don't love ourselves with Christ-confidence.**

    It didn't take long for the prodigal son to go through all the Father had for him, using it on things that were not worth his time. When we don't know that we are worth it, we waste our time continually on things and people who are not worth our time. Interestingly, the New Living Translation calls it wild living. There is only one life down here that God has provided for the believer, and that is the abundant life, according to John 10:10. The wildlife is where we live like we don't respect ourselves even though we think we are. The wildlife is where we go on a shopping spree of revenge – not caring who we hurt in the process. The wildlife is where we forget who we are because of where we are.

Jesus informed us that Satan is a thief who comes to "steal and kill and destroy" (John 10:10, NLT). However, the thief's best way to steal our substance is to get us to give it up. This son got wasted and spent all he had. Jesus came to give him "a rich and satisfying life" (John 10:10, NLT).

Then Christ states, [11] "I am the good shepherd. The good shepherd sacrifices his life for the sheep. [12] A hired hand will run when he sees a wolf coming. He will abandon the sheep because they don't belong to him, and he isn't their shepherd. And so the wolf attacks them and scatters the flock. [13] The hired hand runs away because he's working only for the money and doesn't care about the sheep.[14] "I am the good shepherd; I know my sheep, and they know me, [15] just as my Father knows me and I know the Father. So I sacrifice my life for the sheep. [16] I have other sheep, too, that are not in this sheepfold. I must bring them also. They will listen to my voice, and there will be one flock with one shepherd" (John 10:11-16, NLT).

Jesus makes it clear that he is good for us. Low self-worth is when we don't know what to call good. Insecurity will have us accepting any kind of love because it's better to us than the love we have or never had. The farther the son got from the father's house, the more unloved he felt.

- **Unhealthy attachments.**
  The Bible says that after he wasted his substance and spent all his money, there was a severe recession in the land. Consequently, he attached himself to a citizen, which the New Living Translation says he

"forced himself" on someone to get a job. When looking for love to soothe our thoughts and feelings of low self-worth, we might find ourselves in an unhealthy attachment. We must be careful not to think we have a connection because we have something in common with someone else. One of the signs of having unhealthy self-worth is constantly connecting to others who verbally, emotionally, sexually, physically, and even spiritually abuse us. This is dangerous because being in love with these mindsets will have us trying to "prove ourselves" to them, thinking if they see how good we are to them, they will treat us better. This is not so, my friends. That will make them treat us worse. You deserve better, but by the time you get a thought or clue, they have already convinced you that you need them to survive. No, baby! I need the Lord Jesus Christ to survive and live. It's in Jesus that "we live, and move, and have our being" (Acts 17:28, KJV). The sex may feel like love, but it's not love. After they bruise your eye or hit you in secret, the gifts that others cannot see are not love. This is passive aggressiveness at its best. A nice-nasty if you will.

The best way to get anyone who is insecurely attached to you is to charm them in the beginning or mistreat them in the middle (with a mixture of rewards for being their "servant" and ultimately giving them speeches, gifts, or being charming like they were in the beginning towards the end). This son would have never given him the time of day if he had not left the father's protection. God wants you to know that he is not micromanaging you; He protects you. Don't leave the protection of God to feel free with someone who is designed to kill you. The story tells us that the only thing this unhealthy attachment did for him had him hanging out with the pigs to support himself. Have you been tolerating anyone just to say you have someone? Maybe you still feel dirty after the rape, molestation, or abandonment to the degree to which you have gotten used to someone mistreating and speaking to you in a way that is degrading. Not another day.

- **Glad, but not satisfied.**

It's hard to fill a bucket with a hole in it. Did you notice the Bible shows us that the son was so desperate to get something to eat that he was even glad to eat the pig's lunch? Desperation will make us do things we said we would never normally do. It will have us taking things from people we vowed never to take things from. Believe it or not, unhealthy self-worth manifests itself in being grateful for some kind of love, any kind of attention, or some form of stability. This son was not raised to think, behave, or settle like this. However, if you hang out with pigs long enough, their lunch will eventually look good enough to eat.

A friend of mine told me about a friend she met on Instagram. She was an author, a college graduate, no kids, and emotionally stable. A guy who slid in her DMs was educated, had no kids, and felt entitled. He played mind games with her, and she caught on quickly. So, within the first night of talking to him (which was her only night and last night ever speaking to him again), she simply told him, "I'm not that desperate." She wanted a relationship, but she put in the effort, while being single, to make sure her relationship with herself has self-respect.

"He Came to Himself"

This son had a bed in hell. He went far away from his father. He wasted his savings on wild living and went through a recession after spending all his inheritance. He was given a job feeding pigs (which was considered beneath the Jewish tradition), and the pig's food was starting to look good to him. Then out of nowhere, the Bible says, "He came to himself" (Luke 15:17, KJV).

He remembered he came from royalty. He remembered that he was not raised to settle like he was. He remembered the love of his father. He knew he could go home when he could not go anyplace else. He remembered that he was better than the pigs. He remembered that even the servants back home were eating better than him. He remembered that he was not destined to live self-confidently. He was designed to live Christ-confident.

There is a term in psychology called selective perception. Selective perception means when an individual has an unhealthy view of themselves, they will focus on the two things they believe confirm their thoughts and feelings rather than the five good things about themselves. Therefore it is crucial to be filled with the Holy Spirit. One of the key features of being filled with the Spirit of Christ is that He brings the right thoughts back into our lives. Are you filled with the Holy Spirit?

The Journey to Being Christ-Confident

Finding out who we are in the Lord Jesus Christ is the journey of a lifetime. It doesn't end when we get baptized in the name of Jesus Christ or get filled with the Holy Ghost. It is lifelong progress of continually knowing and trusting in the Jesus you believe (The Jesus of the Bible). Many of us are tired already from the journey we already went on trying to make others love us who could not love themselves.

Many who grew up in the church were baptized in the name of Jesus Christ and filled with the Holy Ghost but have not embraced the Father's love. They have served on various committees in the church but wrestle with the feeling of low self-worth that they are ashamed to discuss.

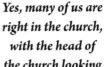

Yes, many of us are right in the church, with the head of the church looking for love in all the wrong places.

Yes, many of us are right in the church, with the head of the church looking for love in all the wrong places.

This boy did not have daddy issues, he never went through church hurt, nor has he ever been in a gang. There was just a need to satisfy the insecure impulse of instant gratification. When we haven't found what or who we wanted in so long, we take anything we can get now. This boy has now lived on both sides of the tracks and decided it is better to be Christ-confident than self-confident. There is a gospel song I like that epitomizes the point I'm making called *There is No Way I Can Make it Without You* by Ricky Dillard. I highly recommend you listen to it.

There are some key points that I want you to understand about the journey back to Christ-confidence that this story affords us with:

1. Repentance & Confession

- This boy knew that he had mistreated his father. He knew that the father was good to him. Nevertheless, he had to fight thoughts of guilt and worthlessness on his way back home. Please don't think it's strange to feel sad after a good prayer. Please don't think it is strange that Christ does not love you after leaving a good church service. And please don't think it's strange that you can be anointed yet feel weak. The scriptures say,

  > "*12 Beloved, do not be surprised at the fiery trial when it comes upon you to test you, as though something strange was happening to you. 13 But rejoice insofar as you share Christ's sufferings, that you may also rejoice and be glad when his glory is revealed. 14 If you are insulted for the name of Christ, you are blessed, because the Spirit of glory[b] and of God rests upon you*" (1 Peter 4:12-14, ESV).

- The enemy does not want us to believe that we can come to God because of our mistakes and past. The enemy doesn't want us to remember that God is married to the backslider. The only thing this boy had going for him was his memory. That is why Satan is after your memory. Unhealthy esteem focuses on what happened, who hurt us, who left us, and who abused us. Unhealthy esteem focuses on the job we didn't get, who we could not have, and the people we loved that did not love us. When I think about the goodness of Jesus and all he's done for me, my soul cries out, Hallelujah! I thank God for saving me.

17 "When he finally came to his senses, he said to himself, 'At home, even the hired servants have food enough to spare, and here I am dying of hunger! 18 I will go home to my father and say, "Father, I have sinned against both heavens, and you, 19 and I am no longer worthy of being called your son. Please take me on as a hired servant."'

20 "So he returned home to his father. And while he was still a long way off, his father saw him coming. Filled with love and compassion, he ran to his son, embraced him, and kissed him. 21 His son said to him, 'Father, I have sinned against both heaven and you, and I am no longer worthy of being called your son.[a]'

22 "But his father said to the servants, 'Quick! Bring the finest robe in the house and put it on him. Get a ring for his finger and sandals for his feet. 23 And kill the calf we have been fattening. We must celebrate with a feast, 24 for my son was dead and has now returned to life. He was lost, but now he is found.' So the party began" (Luke 15:17-24).

Repentance means I turn away from living a self-confident life and start living a Christ-confident life. I turn from doing things my way and living the way the Lord Jesus Christ wants me to live. The enemy's trick is to have us so comfortable in our sins and self-loathing that we continue to sit on unconfessed sins. However, the book is clear: if we confess and forsake our sins, God is faithful to forgive (1 John 1:8-9).

2. Embrace What Christ Has to Offer

- So many of us are so used to losing that we don't know when we are winning. The son was trying to finish his speech, but did you see the father cut him off? The father was ready to forgive him. I want you to know that we must be aware of the fight that Christ is ready to forgive to be Christ-confident. He doesn't want our iniquities to separate us from him (Isaiah 59:2).

- The father only gave the son what he gave up! Read that twice. God wants to give you what he already had for you that you already gave up on. Maybe you gave up on love because someone gave up on you. Maybe you gave up on the dream Christ put in your heart because you don't have the financial means to get your career off the ground. God doesn't keep anything back from those who walk upright before him, according to Psalms 84:11.

- I think that many of us are more accepting of God's stuff than God's love. Now I'm not saying you're a God-digger, but I am saying that when we lose trust in the love of the people we have been chasing, we give up on the greatest love of all: God's love. Please do yourself a favor: don't give up on God's love. Jesus is love. You will need love when life gets crazy, people act funny, banks are lazy, and loyalty becomes odd.

Learning to be Ignored: You Don't Have to Be Celebrated by Everyone

Studies show that giving someone silent treatment is equivalent to causing someone physical pain. The best way to mentally torment a prisoner in the prison system is to place them in solitary confinement. It's not just women who don't like being ignored. Men and children hate it too. However, being insecure makes them question who they are. When the son returned home, the father threw a big party to celebrate. The only problem was his blood brother did not want to come inside.

> [25] *"Meanwhile, the older son was in the fields working. When he returned home, he heard music and dancing in the house,* [26] *and he asked one of the servants what was going on.* [27] *'Your brother is back,' he was told, 'and your father has killed the fattened calf. We are celebrating because of his safe return.'*
>
> [28] *"The older brother was angry and wouldn't go in. His father came out and begged him,* [29] *but he replied, 'All these years I've slaved for you and never once refused to do a single thing you told me to. And in all that time, you never gave me even one young goat for a feast with my friends.* [30] *Yet when this son of yours comes back after squandering your money on prostitutes, you celebrate by killing the fattened calf!'*
>
> [31] *"His father said to him, 'Look, dear son, you have always stayed by me, and every-*

thing I have is yours. ³² We had to celebrate this happy day. For your brother was dead and has come back to life! He was lost, but now he is found" (Luke 15:25-32, NLT).

When we have struggled with low self-worth most of our lives, we have anxiety (a self-esteem attack) when it comes to our celebrations. Many have held up their lives waiting on someone to say congratulations, and it's not coming. Many have let go of true love, going back to old flames that only burn up their self-image, sending their confidence up in flames.

Now the father in the story represents God. The older brother represents the self-righteous who hold your past against you, and, of course, the boy who left home represents you, and I. God gave a celebration, and the older brother didn't come. He has a problem with God forgiving the son who went out there. Many have a problem with the Lord Jesus Christ, God Almighty himself, for blessing you.

Why are you trying to win someone over who does not care if they lose you?

Ironically, when we look at this story again, we see nowhere that the younger son, who messed up, went outside to beg the brother to come in. I want to ask you the question, **"Why are you trying to win someone over who does not care if they lose you?"**

No More Guilt Trips

As the old sayings go, "If you don't know who you are, anyone can fool you, rule you, and control you." The boy messed up, left the father, and probably didn't say goodbye to his older brother. However, he will not allow his brother's behavior to talk him into giving up on what the father gave him. **Stop arguing with people over what the Father gave you.**

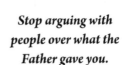

For some people to control us with guilt, they have to know us like the back of their hand. They have to study us or get us to talk, learn our secrets, or catch us at vulnerable

Stop arguing with people over what the Father gave you.

moments in our lives. For some, this started in childhood. I never will forget a client that we will call Todd, who had a highly manipulative father. His dad had four children, and he was the oldest.

Todd's father was headed to law school, but his mother got pregnant with Todd. His father made it clear to Todd that he would have been an attorney by now "if I didn't choose to put my life aside for you." Todd has become increasingly insecure, thinking that things are his fault. So, as a result, Todd became a loner for most of his life, not asking for help, not wanting to be a burden. Although Todd's father never told Todd that he regretted being his dad, that's precisely what he was implying.

Consequently, when Todd's father wanted to borrow money, he would clean out his son's account, using the "I put my dreams aside for you" guilt trip. Todd would get angry with his dad because he was aware of his father's tactics but didn't know how to relinquish the feelings of guilt. Todd had to learn three things that I am going to share with you now:

• Set Boundaries With These Mindsets

Should Todd respect his father? Absolutely! Should Todd check on his father? Absolutely! Should Todd keep going broke because his father (who can still go to law school) uses guilt against him? No! Todd may have to limit the visits or have a conversation with his father (Todd's dad did not believe his son had the boldness to call him out). Remember, what we tolerate continues.

- Love Yourself as Much as You Love Them

Todd loved his father, but ever since he heard his father's remarks from his childhood, he had a hard time loving himself. Often, we tolerate more than we would like to from our family because they are family. However, to sit on unresolved issues will do more harm than good.

- Not Standing up for Yourself Will Hurt More Than the Hurt They Have Already Inflicted on You

This is going to keep happening until you say something; you are going to keep feeling weak, secretly resentful, depressed, insecure, and angry because you won't say anything. Christ-confidence is more than speaking to ourselves in a Christ-like way; it's also about going to our loved ones and telling them what lovingly bothers us. I repeat, this will keep happening to you until you love yourself with Christ-confidence. Don't you want to be free?

PART 4

Finally, Jesus

CHAPTER
EIGHT

I Have to Stop Chasing People

"Did I ever ask you for anything! Did I ever ask
you for anything! I never asked you for anything.
Not even your sorry hand in marriage."
—Celie

I will never forget reading a heartbreaking story about
a man who was highly into a woman who was not
suitable for him. We will call him Jarrod. He had met
a woman who was beautiful, charming, and very street smart.
Jarrod was twenty-seven with no kids. She was thirty-two with
one daughter. Jarrod was a landscaper with no kids raised by
a single mother who taught him to respect women. She was
raised by her aunt and uncle, who took her in at eleven when
her parents were gunned down in a drive-by shooting.

However, her uncle was highly addicted to cocaine, and
her aunt was barely home. Her aunt was a nurse that worked
double shifts to support the family. Her husband was using
all his money to buy drugs. Well, one night, he was high
and raped his niece. We will call her Ranay. She left home at
fourteen and never looked back. She vowed to get every man
back since "they only want one thing."

All her relationships were only with men she could control. When they grew tired of her ways, they left her, and she went on to the next victim. Jarrod, the man who grew up in southern hospitality, was unaware of this. Subsequently, she knew he was inexperienced in the city. In Brooklyn, where she grew up, she told him she would show him around the city. He did not realize that he was about to be the next victim in her horror story.

After a few dates, where she made him pay for dinner at many expensive restaurants, bought her the latest designer bags, and paid for all her daughter's shopping sprees, she gave him a sad story about how she was about to get put out of her house (she was staying with her other man). Within three months, he moved her into a lavish apartment, an island in the kitchen, big-screen TVs, and a king-sized bed. She felt like she finally found the perfect man (the perfect victim). Little did he know, he bought the apartment for her and her new man.

Well, one day, he came by to see her on his break, and as he opened the door, she was on the living room sofa, having sex with her other man and her female friend. Yes, they were having a threesome. Jarrod lost his cool, beginning to scream at the top of his lungs. "How could you do this to me! I take care of your daughter, who I see as my own. I bought you an apartment and these big screens TVs. I would have never cheated on you (with tears running down his face). She looked him in the face, with the calmest tone, and said, "I never asked you to."

I'm a Sucker for Love

I know your heart must have gone out to Jarrod as you read his story. I know Ranay's insensitivity and lack of remorse for Jarrod bothered you. Yes, this woman was a street-intelligent city girl, who knew how to play the game, and chose the most innocent person to scam. Jarrod was only trying to love her. That's all he wanted to do. He had no ulterior motives. Did he have the opportunity to meet other women who would have treated him right? Absolutely! However, Ranay was the only woman he wanted. We want what we want, do we?

"I'm a sucker for love," Jarrod says. He grew up around love, hugs, and family dinners. He grew up around a mother who encouraged him to talk about his feelings. However, there are psychological undertones of this kind-hearted fellow. He is a pawn in the hands of the wrong woman because he is trying not to disappoint another Black woman the way his father disappointed his mother.

I'm Trying to Be Who You Want Me to Be

Jarrod's mother, Nancy, was left to raise her son herself after her husband was caught sleeping around with her sister, Meagan. Since Jarrod was her only child and the "man of the house now" (he was only nine), he had to listen to his mother constantly vent about her anger, rage, sadness, insecurities, and bitterness towards her sister, especially the father. You would think that she would be more upset with the sister. However, this is the second time her sister has done this to her. She opened up to her husband about what her sister did. He vowed never to be alone in one room with her sister. Nancy's trust is destroyed.

Jarrod experienced this all at just nine years old. He spent his childhood thinking he had to clean up his father's mess. So, he developed what I call "a male nurturer's heart." If he meets a woman he thinks has it all together, he leaves her because she does not need nurturing. He only feels comforted with women he has to take care of the way he did his mom. In an endeavor not to be like his father, he is not being who he truly is. He has not discovered who he is. Kindness is his role, but secretly he does not know how to be kind to himself.

This Goes Out to All Jarrod's

There are many people like Jarrod out there who are battling with low self-worth in the name of love. It's to the degree to which you are allowing someone else's insecurity to cause you to doubt what you bring to the table and the love that you have to offer. Here are seven lessons we can learn from "Jarrod Syndrome."

1. **Not Everyone Is Looking for Love**

   Listen, I know you love him or her, and you have a nurturing heart. You don't want to see them hurt, but they were not raised with love. They were raised hurt. When people have been raised hurt, they don't know how to live. So, they just learn to survive. They no longer see the world as a safe place. They have trust issues that stem from their childhood that cause them to hurt those who come into their lives in adulthood. However, your love is big! Your heart is big, but their love isn't even tiny. They don't even love themselves. They never planned on loving you, which *does not mean* you are not lovable. You saw a beautiful person that you wanted to treat like royalty. They see a broken person who is out to get revenge on others. They don't believe in love, but please don't allow it to affect how you love.

2. **It's Not Your Responsibility to Heal Your Mother or Anyone**

I once heard someone say, "I don't need you to fix me. I need you to love me while I fix myself." Your mother (or parents) meant well, but they may have treated you as one of their girlfriends or boyfriends, putting a lot of emotional weight on you. You were carrying your mom when she should have been carrying you. This thought pattern has caused you to think that you only love if you carry broken people.

The only problem with that is if you carry a broken person, who is hurting others on purpose, they will put you down when they are ready. There is nothing wrong with being a gentleman or gentlewoman; there is something wrong with being a Savior. Only Jesus can save us. The more you try to rescue others, the more you start drowning yourself.

3. **You Can't Expect Whole Love from People Who Don't Understand Love**

It is not that people don't love us as much as the lack of love they don't have for themselves. We expect too much of ourselves from people when the goal is to expect respect. Don't expect the love of anyone who doesn't respect you. Respect is love in action. You loved someone that didn't respect you. So, the question is, do you respect yourself? When we respect ourselves, people don't look good if they aren't good for us.

4. **You Date on the Level of Your Self-Esteem**

The person saw great qualities in you. They saw the desire to help them in you. Also, trust and believe me when I tell you that they also saw your insecurities. They were intensely aware that you did not love yourself. There is an old saying: "I refuse to be a part of a club that would have me as a member." That means when individuals see themselves as small, they lose respect for anyone who sees them as significant. Due to their lack of trust, they think you want something from them or patronize them. Both of you have unhealthy self-esteem. However, they played the role of the dominant insecure one in the relationship.

In contrast, you play the role of the submissive insecure one in the relationship. Don't you know that you are better than that? That's not complementing each other. That's not opposites attract. The both of you had more in common than you realized at the time. That was an imbalance. Our love cannot make someone love themselves. That's the effort they have to put in for themselves, and don't you forget that.

5. **You Leave Later Rather Than Sooner**
This person was willing to ride this thing out. They barely did anything for you. They did not care to meet your family. They only wanted what they could get out of you. They did not believe the warranty on the relationship, manipulation, and control could not expire. Some individuals are indeed going to drag you along as long as you allow them to. I'd rather be respected than loved any day. Just because someone stays with you does not mean they are loyal to you. **Sometimes they stay because they know that you aren't going to leave.**

Hear me good. They knew you were not going to leave. That's why they did not leave their secret lovers and had a threesome with them. The good news is you did not marry them.

Sometimes they stay because they know that you aren't going to leave.

6. **Ask the Lord Jesus Christ to Heal You, Not Them**

It is normal to miss them. That means you have a heart. **What is not normal is thinking we want the toxicity that we miss. When our esteem is low, we often run back to the person who left us for comfort. Jesus told us if we won't rest, we have to come to him— not anyone else. Rest now before you decide to love again.** It's like the kid who loves the mother in the house but still wants to contact the father who never showed up in their life. We are social creatures. I get it. However, it's like the drug user on cocaine, thinking that the next time he sniffs cocaine, he won't get high. Nothing from nothing leaves nothing. Remember that.

7. **It's Never About Anyone Else but You**

You were not responsible for how your mom chose to raise you the first half of your life, but you are responsible for what you choose to do with the second half of your life. Your girlfriend has hurt you, but you have allowed her to. Never allow yourself to accept that kind of abuse ever again, and I mean never again.

NINE

The Secret Behind Manipulation

> "I don't get played; I play along. I play
> my games by playing your game"
> —Anonymous

*D*id you think we were going to skip this topic? The devil lied to you. We cannot talk about going from self-confident to Christ-confident without first discussing the elephant in the room. You know what I'm talking about—playing sick when you don't want your husband to visit his side of the family. You answer the phone laughing and then say hello to make your spouse jealous and paranoid. You know how you do.

We have to talk about manipulation because it has you thinking you're ahead of the game. You have become so egotistical that you stay with a manipulator that you know plays games. However, you make time in your life to waste more time with these foolish shenanigans due to the bitterness you carry in your heart. God wants you healed, my friend, and he wants you healed and set free right now in the name of the Lord Jesus Christ!

I will never forget a friend of mine who meant no harm but did a lot of damage. She was a master manipulator. I mean, good at the game. And I mean really good. She grew up being told that men could not be trusted. When you grow up hearing something all your life, you can't help but believe it. As she navigated her way through high school, she saw how guys would play games with her female friends. Mind you; she already saw her brothers cheat on women.

Additionally, she was already traumatized by her "con artist of a dad." She was angry after hearing her mother's side of the story of how he hit her when she was only three years old. She was determined that this would not be her.

Manipulators are living in a prison of discouragement. Let me give you my definition of discouragement: **Discouragement is when you have seen so much wrong go in your life to the degree to which you think you have seen it all.** My friend checked out of life before she could even get up on her feet. The only hope she believed she had at finding Mr. Almost (She didn't believe in Mr. Right) was to make him. The problem with that is she forgot that Jesus Christ is the only Creator. Besides the Lord Jesus Christ, there is no other God. Colossians 1:15 teaches us that Jesus Christ made all things!!

The moment we think we can make someone into who we want them to be is a dead giveaway that we are insecure about who Jesus Christ has called us to be. Reread

Discouragement is when you have seen so much wrong go in your life to the degree to which you think you have seen it all.

The moment we think we can make someone into who we want them to be is a dead giveaway that we are insecure about who Jesus Christ has called us to be.

this, slowly. She is almost in her forties and is still being left by every man she tries to make. The only problem with her creations is that she can't make them stay. She never allowed Jesus Christ to make her Christ-confident. Salvation is not about God changing who we want to manipulate. God is not going to help us manipulate anyone. Salvation is about Christ changing us.

I counseled another woman who said to me, "I fix my man's car seat so that I can tell if another woman has been in my car. His last girlfriend broke him down, and I built him up into the man that I wanted him to be." The only problem with that is that if she built him up, another woman could remake him. You see, manipulation has an irrational way of thinking, "I got this." Now let's do some digging.

The Anxiety of Manipulation

All manipulators are highly anxious at the core. They fear the subsequent heartbreak, the next backstabber, or the next failed relationship. To them, if they think the worst, it won't happen. If they leave room for disappointment, it won't hurt as much. They are unaware that leaving room for disappointment creates a mansion for disappointment. Why? They will always act like the person they think they are. It's not the fear of failure; it's feeling like a failure that is the battle.

Remember, we stated earlier that anxiety is a manifestation of low self-esteem. A manipulator has deep-seated insecurities that they aren't good enough; doing the right things will produce the results they want in the long run. They have gone beyond trying to help God out. They simply want to do it their way and then invite God to bless it. If God chooses not to bless their scheme, they will say, "so be it. I got this." No, my friend, your insecurities have you.

Back to Ranay

You remember Ranay from chapter eight, don't you? She broke Jarrod's heart by being caught in a threesome when he came to see her on his lunch break? Well, in the last chapter, we gave some advice to Jarrod. In this chapter, I want to talk to Ranay and all who have Ranays similar problems. Ranay doesn't need us to beat her down. She needs someone to see past the damage she has done and the heartbreak she caused and tell her the truth in love. Here is the conversation I had with her:

Curtis: God loves you. You are more precious to Jesus Christ than you realize. I didn't come here to make you feel put down or attacked. However, I want you to know that you have lost so much trust in men that you have given up on yourself. The only ones you care to be with are the emotionally unavailable ones. Jesus did not allow himself to be nailed to a cross so that you can nail yourself to unavailable men. You mentioned to me that you are bisexual. You only deal with women because you don't trust men. Do you know what God's love feels like?

Ranay: Does it look like I know what God's love feels like? If he loved me, he would not have allowed it to happen to me! I know you're trying to help me but, look! It's a lot of layers to me.

Curtis: Do you feel like nobody understands where you're coming from?

Ranay: Exactly! Everyone sees what I did. Did they see the blood leaking from my legs when my nasty drunk of a skunk uncle raped me?

Curtis: Do you mind telling me how you felt after the rape?

Ranay: Angry. I'm still angry. I feel like nothing, and that's exactly how I made Jarrod and every man in my life try to make me feel the opposite.

Curtis: Do you feel like you would have treated others better if you had healthier self-worth?

Ranay: Well, duh. I'm sorry for getting snappy with you. It's just that it's a lot.

Curtis: Would you like to end our session for today?

Ranay: No, I'm ok. We can finish. I want to know more about healthy self-esteem. I made many mistakes, but I do have faith in Jesus. My friends told me you could help me. Yeah, I'm a tough cookie, but I had to be.

Curtis: I have one more question for today's session.

Ranay: Ok

Curtis: What do you get out of the games you play with the guys who are good to you?

Ranay: Everything! I get it all. I get to twist their hearts, and I get their money. I get to decide when it's over. I get to decide when we have sex. I get to decide what I want to eat even it he is allergic to the food. I know it sounds mean, but the truth sets you free, right?

Curtis: I understand. However, I do believe that you're after these men to get everything because you think you're nothing.

Ranay bursts into tears and walks out. Seven minutes later, she comes back.

Ranay: I hate to think about this stuff. When I went out for a smoke, I realized that I get a fake feeling of feeling good about myself because I feel in control. I screamed, kicked, and fought my uncle, but he was just too strong. I feel like a weak chick. I'm drained

Curtis: Maybe you still feel weak because you never relied on Christ's strength in the areas of your pain.

Ranay: I mean, I went to church. I still go. I sing in the choir, and the girl he caught me with is the choir director.

Curtis: What you just described are the jobs and committees we have in the church. I'm talking about a real relationship with Jesus Christ, where he walks with you and talks with you and tells you that you are his own?

Ranay: God doesn't want to walk with me. When I go to church, I keep my distance away.

Curtis: So, are you saying you go to the house of God without trying to get close to the man of the house?

Ranay: I guess I messed that up, too.

Curtis: No, what is messed up is not seeing yourself the way Christ sees you. You have been through trauma that you haven't coped with healthily. Your self-worth has taken a hit. You have been in survival mode every since the rape from your uncle. You coped with it by teaching yourself to build up emotional walls to control the good and chase unavailable men. You don't want a commitment, but you did want to get back that sense of control.

That has caused you to sabotage every relationship with the good men, like Jarrod. God wants you to know that he loves you. He knows all about the rape, lies, the manipulation, and all. He has always watched over you, but He wants to be inside you.

You've committed to church but not a genuine commitment to him. We often try to hide our brokenness because we think it's a stigma, but Jesus came to heal the brokenhearted.

You have been so hurt that you've tried everything to numb the pain. Your options have been so open to healing the pain you've tried another woman. Jesus doesn't want you in that lifestyle. He wants you whole.

Ranay: I tried Jesus too!

Curtis: Don't try Jesus; trust Jesus.

Ranay: How do I get right with God? I don't know what to say.

Curtis: Coming back to God requires obeying him and trusting him in areas that hurt. The Bible says we must repent, be baptized in the name of Jesus Christ to forgive our sins, and Christ will feel us with the Holy Spirit (Acts 2:38).

Ranay: My church doesn't do that.

Curtis: My pastor does. Come over this Sunday, and we will gladly baptize you in the name of Jesus Christ.

Come to Jesus and Give Up the Games

Many of us are baptized in Jesus Christ's name and filled with the Holy Ghost but struggle with trust. We have reduced the faith to just believing in Christ for a new job, career, house, or spouse but haven't trusted Christ with our secrets and pain, trauma, abandonment, and neglect. When we trust Jesus Christ, we lay our manipulation tactics at His feet.

Can You Locate Your Tactics On the List Below?

Ranay played a lot of games. Go through the manipulation list and see which one applies to you.

- Not calling them first to see if they call you
- Telling them to go when you want them to stay

- Comparing how much more attention they give someone else than you
- Using guilt to get them to give you what you want
- Giving them the silent treatment
- Not confronting the person who hurt you but making subliminal Facebook posts about them
- Hiding the keys when your husband gets ready to leave the house
- Using sex as a weapon
- Talking loudly to intimidate others to give in to your wishes
- Trying to turn others against those you're mad at
- Playing dumb

These are just a few manipulative tactics that we use as defense mechanisms to calm the anxieties that stem from our insecurities to keep ourselves from experiencing any further pain. These are the tactics of manipulation. However, there is only one reason for manipulation: low self-esteem.

Low Self-Esteem is the Mastermind Behind Manipulation

Often, when we think of manipulation, we may automatically think of someone in a high position, a gold digger, or an abusive husband. I have even seen manipulation in church. I've seen good ole-saved wives hide the mail from their husbands on the deacon board. I've seen manipulation among parents who have manipulated their child for information about the other parent.

Manipulation is low self-worth coming through the back door to get what they want instead of just asking the

Savior to help them, realizing they can do all things through Christ that strengthens them. A manipulator does not believe that anyone will help them, so they believe "if you want it done, you have to do it yourself."

The manipulation is mismanaged insecurities. You have become depressed and anxious somewhere along the way because you feel like nothing goes your way. Nevertheless, we don't realize that things are not supposed to go our way. Jesus is the way, the truth, and the life (John 14:6). The sooner we embrace that, Christ-confidence will change our lives.

Hidden Agendas

[6] While I was at the window of my house, looking through the curtain, [7] I saw some naive young men, and one in particular who lacked common sense. [8] He was crossing the street near the house of an immoral woman, strolling down the path by her house. [9] It was at twilight, in the evening, as deep darkness fell. [10] The woman approached him, seductively dressed and sly of heart. [11] She was the brash, rebellious type, never content to stay home. [12] She is often in the streets and markets, soliciting at every corner. [13] She threw her arms around him. She kissed him, and with a bold look, she said, [14] «I've just made my peace offerings and fulfilled my vows. [15] You're the one I was looking for! I came out to find you, and here you are! [16] My bed is spread with beautiful blankets, with colored sheets of Egyptian linen. [17] I've perfumed my bed

with myrrh, aloes, and cinnamon. [18] Come, let›s drink our fill of love until morning. Let›s enjoy each other›s caresses, [19] for my husband is not home. He›s away on a long trip. [20] He has taken a wallet full of money with him and won›t return until later this month. "[21] So she seduced him with her pretty speech and enticed him with her flattery. [22] He followed her at once, like an ox going to the slaughter. He was like a stag caught in a trap, [23] awaiting the arrow that would pierce its heart. He was like a bird flying into a snare, little knowing it would cost him his life.

[24] So listen to me, my sons, and pay attention to my words. [25] Don›t let your hearts stray away toward her. Don›t wander down her wayward path. [26] For she has been the ruin of many; many men have been her victims. [27] Her house is the road to the grave. Her bedroom is the den of death" (Proverbs 7:6-27, NLT).

There are some things in the above passage that are profound. This woman said all the right things for all the wrong reasons. She was spoiled by a good man but appeared not satisfied. While running the show, she knows how to make a naive man feel like a wise man. Let's be clear all manipulators are not women; men are too.

We frequently forget that whatever we do to get up, we must also do to stay up. Many of us are still hurting over someone's manipulative behavior tactics. When someone has low self-worth, it doesn't just affect them, but it hurts everyone around them who is trying to love them. Keep in mind the manipulator is not always aware that they have low self-worth, but they are aware of what they are doing to you.

When we have hidden agendas, it's not fair to the people who have come into our lives to love us. People are not mind readers. The expectation is too high to expect someone to play the role of Christ in our lives. Often, the person on the receiving end of the hidden agenda did not know there was one until the person who set them up lashed out, suddenly stopped answering the phone, or gave them the silent treatment.

Then Say That!

Manipulators are not very good communicators. If they communicate, the game is over. They keep you guessing, leave you in the dark, and then play dumb when they're called out. Keep in mind this manipulator could be you. Manipulators want the same thing honest individuals want. However, they are not good at communicating, and they believe if they talk too much, you'll see their insecurities. There are three destructive styles of communication that I would like to address:

Manipulators are not very good communicators.

A-Passive Communication

Latasha wants Jerry to spend time with her, but she passively cooks him big meals instead of telling him. She wears his favorite perfume around the house on days she knows he wants to hang out with the guys. Although Jerry enjoys the food and compliments her fragrance, he blows her kisses as he heads out the door to see his friends.

B-Passive-Aggressive Communication

Latasha wants Jerry to spend time with her, but instead of communicating that, she smiles, blows him a kiss back, and calls her ex to come over and help her try on outfits. However, she makes him leave before her husband gets back. Jerry comes home and sees two wine glasses on the sofa.

When he approaches her and asks her, "Why are there two wine glasses out?"

She jokingly says, "I have them out for us silly," and walks away, saying to herself, "Now he wants to act like he is paying attention."

C-Aggressive Communication

Latasha wants Jerry to spend time with her. Still, instead of verbalizing her feelings effectively, she yells at him after he calmly asks what's for dinner, "When you stay home and stop hanging out with your ugly friends, you might get some fish sticks at least!"

All three ways of communicating are bad for her marriage. However, many who battle with low self-esteem don't like being rejected, ignored, and not being attended to. Many marriages have failed not due to cheating but because someone was not communicating how they feel. It takes courage to say what we need to say.

Assertive Communication

Latisha wants Jerry to spend the weekend with her. She waits until he is settling in and commends him on being a good husband. She tells him how thankful she is that he spends all those long hours at work to make a life for her and the kids. Then she verbalizes, "I miss us spending time together. Let's set a date in the next two weeks for just us. What do you think?"

Jerry heard the love in his wife's voice say that she missed him in her body language. He agreed and took her out tonight.

Self-Confident vs. Christ-Confidence

Self-confidence is all about relying on self to get the job done. Self-confident individuals may not manipulate until they get desperate enough. That's the dangerous thing about being led by self. Self does not always know how far to go and when to leave. However, Christ-confident knows that godliness with contentment is significant (1 Timothy 6:6, KJV). Ranay had a false self-confidence that made her feel in control for a while. Still, after the conversation, she learned that Christ-confidence is the key to overcoming manipulation.

It's a Lonely Game

Playing these mind games on others to ease our feelings of inferiority will do more harm than good in the long run. People get tired and eventually leave. You may be saying, "they can go if they want to go. I have been hurt before." That defense mechanism gets real old fast. It hurts us in the end. Sooner or later, we have to comply with God's will for our lives. **Jesus Christ wants us to have life abundantly.**

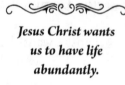

Jesus Christ wants us to have life abundantly.

Only a Game Gets Played

I saw a guy on Instagram say that "Deep down inside, we know who is really for us. When someone is for you, they are calling on you, checking on you. They're not asking what *you* are doing. They are asking what *we* are doing. You can't play games with someone who is not a game. Only games get played. Even a dog knows who loves them."

You may be saying, "No, bro! I have been played." Let me tell you, when God has a plan for your life; you're not played. You're preserved. God can use every heartbreak to bring glory to himself. Make up your mind to set boundaries in your life, not allow others to play games with you, and don't play games with anyone else. Learn to ask for what you want but know who to ask. Don't ask those who can't give. Don't ask those who are cold towards you. Christ has already given you people who love you, but you will never embrace them if you continue to allow yourself to chase after those who fuel your low self-worth.

CHAPTER
TEN

Body Image Issues

"So, you must honor God with your body."
—the apostle Paul

I don't think the world heard her when she said, "I am not my hair; I am the soul that lives within." I'm talking about singer India Arie. She is known for her classy, graceful, and smooth vocals and her confidence as an African American woman. We have been conditioned to believe that we can think and feel better about ourselves if we decorate the outside in our Western culture. This is the danger of applying self-confidence to the exterior.

Swag

Swag is a term from our millennials that means someone is excellent and has a personality. Swag is not an evil word; it's what we use it for that is the problem. Wanting to look good is something that we all aspire to, but our self-esteem will take a hit if we look for what we wear to make us feel better about ourselves. Children go to school and compare what they have to what others have. Then, after getting picked on, they talk their parents into buying what other kids in their school have.

It carries on into adulthood, where you were happy with your major in college until someone else tried to downplay your educational pursuits, so you changed your major. It also goes into relationships, where you have someone who treats you like the queen you are, but he isn't up to your parents' and friends' standards. Let me tell you about real swag:

1. **Swag has nothing to do with anyone's opinion of you.**

   Often, we are vulnerable and fall victim to the opinions of others, especially when they are the voices of those that we love. We want to live our lives, but our insecurity is preoccupied, simultaneously, with disappointing them. We don't want them to tell us what to do, but we want them to approve of what we do. That's not swag; that unhealthy self-worth. Real swagger is all about being comfortable in your skin without being preoccupied with the thoughts of others.

2. **Swag is not a competition.**

   Real swag isn't trying to outdo your brother, have more kids than your sister. Real swag is not trying to start a business because your friends started a business. Bishop T. D. Jakes once stated, "When you define success

Once you have tapped into Christ-confidence, you'll never want to go back to self-confidence.

as beating someone else, they become the benchmark that you live by." I have no desire to preach the next preacher out. I have no desire to outwrite the next author. **Once you have tapped into Christ-confidence, you'll never want to go back to self-confidence.**

I Like What You Have On

Will Smith stated, "We spend money we don't have, to buy things we don't need, to impress people we don't like." We have purchased items that have put us in financial hardship in order to impress others. I will never forget this girl in elementary school trying to impress this guy who was interested in another girl. He did not pay her any mind. So, she fought the girl he liked. One day, she couldn't take any more. She went to him crying, letting him know that she fought another girl for him and "you still don't want me." One day, he told us, "I don't like either one of them. I just like what she has on."

Love the Skin You're In

I counseled a woman who had deep insecurities because her mother called her sister prettier than her. She was good at academics, so she used her education to put her sister down. When it came to dating, she only dated men she felt smarter than. She was loved for her intelligence but did not love her skin. I want to take time to address some areas of body image.

Light Skin vs. Black Skin

This is still a topic of discussion to this day. It's still discussed on social media and talk shows; it's still one of the core conflicts of low self-esteem, especially for dark-skinned women. I remember growing up hearing the pain of women who felt ugly because of their dark skin. Men, please stop telling our dark-skinned sisters, "You're cute for a dark-skinned girl."

That has left them with a sense of insecurity that you will never understand. For our African American men: Back in the day, dark men were seen as thugs, gangsters, and overall frightening. Today dark skin is in.

However, a dark-skinned man still had luck with women. They would describe him as tall, dark, and handsome. However, that does not mean lighter-skinned men or women are not affected. I know some light-skinned men who wished they were darker because now it seems darker-skinned men are making a comeback. I have known light-skinned women who have tried not to sound too proper so that the darker-skinned woman would not think they are acting white. Light skin and dark skin are both acceptable to God.

Plastic Surgery

Who can forget the timeless sermon, No More Sheets, preached by Dr. Juanita Bynum? She openly discussed her multiple affairs with men in the church, struggle with sex, and dating the wrong men. She touched the hearts of countless women that night with a raw truth that assisted them with the underlying low self-worth that they were facing. Well fast forward a few years. She openly confessed on national television that she had had plastic surgery. It shocked the church circle.

The church world was not ready to embrace the plastic surgery business because it was considered not of God. However, you want to know what's not of God: insecurity. It came from the enemy. We are not preaching to the insecurity in the pews. Unfortunately, many who have low self-esteem have covered it up with a title, robe, or position in the church. The former President of the United States of America, Abraham Lincoln, said, "If you want to test a man's character, give him power." However, the character is predicated on self-worth.

It's Just My Imagination

Our self-image is predicated on the pictures we paint in our heads. The Bible puts it this way:

> *Our self-image is predicated on the pictures we paint in our heads.*

> *"3 For though we walk in the flesh, we do not war after the flesh:*
> *4 (For the weapons of our warfare are not carnal, but mighty through God to the pulling down of strongholds;)*
> *5 Casting down imaginations, and every high thing that exalteth itself against the knowledge of God, and bringing into captivity every thought to the obedience of Christ;" (2 Corinthians 10:3-5, KJV).*

Interestingly, the Greek word for imagination is reasoning. Psychologists just call it the internal dialogue. It's not how we look that makes us hate our appearance. It's not even the teasing in school that makes us have insecurities about ourselves. It is the reasoning or the self-talk that we have with ourselves. If you want to change your self-image, change how you talk to yourself.

You Can Only Live for Christ

According to God's word, God made us for his glory by making us in his image. Satan hates that. Remember, Satan wanted to be God. So, anyone who is made in the image of God is on Satan's hit list. And when you love yourself for who you are in Christ, that aggravates Satan more. Let Satan be aggravated, and Christ be exalted.

If you take a moment right now to do some reflecting, you'll realize that most of your pain, struggles, betrayals, and heartbreak has their roots in how you see yourself. When you are created to live for Christ, you will not fit in with others, be liked by all, and be invited to every function. You're called to stand out, not be invited out. And you have to be ok with that. Living to please Jesus Christ will not have you accepted by everyone, but God will send people who love you for the image Christ made you in.

Sexually Transmitted Diseases

12 You say, "I am allowed to do anything," —but not everything is good for you. And even though "I am allowed to do anything," I must not become a slave to anything. 13 You say, "Food was made for the stomach, and the stomach for food." (This is true, though some-

day God will do away with both of them.) But you can't say that our bodies were made for sexual immorality. They were made for the Lord, and the Lord cares about our bodies. [14] *And God will raise us from the dead by his power, just as he raised our Lord from the dead.*

[15] Don't you realize that your bodies are parts of Christ? Should a man take his body, which is part of Christ, and join it to a prostitute? Never! [16] *And don't you realize that if a man joins himself to a prostitute, he becomes one body with her? For the Scriptures say, "The two are united into one."[d]* [17] *But the person who is joined to the Lord is one spirit with him.*

[18] Run from sexual sin! No other sin so clearly affects the body as this one does. Sexual immorality is a sin against your own body. [19] *Don't you realize that your body is the temple of the Holy Spirit, who lives in you and was given to you by God? You do not belong to yourself,* [20] *for God bought you a high price. So, you must honor God with your body"* (1 Corinthians 6:12-20, NLT).

That's an exciting passage, isn't it? Apostle Paul writes to the early church about taking care of their bodies. To do this, he uses examples that can make the body better or worse:

1- FOOD

Food can be an addiction. It was here before crack, cocaine, or pain medication. Many of us can change our lives and improve our health by watching what and how much and what we place on our plates. Hypertension, diabetes, cholesterol, and heart disease are the consequences of not taking care of our bodies. Paul teaches us that the sense of entitlement also makes us think that we can consume grease, fatty foods, and soda that won't catch up with us later.

2- FORNICATION

Let's be clear; he isn't speaking on marriage. The Bible clearly shows us that the marriage bed is undefiled, according to Hebrews 13:4. He is speaking of having sex with anyone before marriage in an endeavor to feel good about ourselves for the moment. Sex will make us feel attracted, wanted, and desired, but it can't make us accept ourselves for who we are in Christ.

God does not want us to have sex with anyone because sleeping around with the wrong one attaches our soul to them, having us become one. I have heard many Christians say they don't believe in soul ties, but according to the above passage, we become one with the person we sleep with. A sign that you have slept with the wrong individual is that you begin to feel insecure about yourself the longer you stay with them; you have cursed others out for telling you that you deserve better; you fight to prove your worth to them and still feel unappreciated; regardless of what you do, it's never enough; they have you on a back-and-forth roller coaster ride.

You are Not Up for Sale

Notice, Paul reminds the church at Corinth who was having orgies, incest, and constantly sleeping around with each other that God already purchased them. Their body belongs to God. Jesus Christ values your body more than you realize. You are not for sale. Christ purchased your body with his blood. When we treat our bodies accordingly, the love of Christ overshadows us. Don't allow anyone to compromise that. God already purchased you. Walk like you're worthy.

Present Your Body a Living Sacrifice

The Bible teaches us to present our bodies to God as a living sacrifice, holy and acceptable unto God, which is our reasonable service, according to Romans 12:1. That's why the enemy does not want us to take care of our bodies. Satan does not mind us eating everything and having sex with anyone because he does not want us to be presentable unto God. The body wants what it wants. The body is concerned with its wishes, needs, and wants.

The only way to present my body to God is to be Christ-confident when hunger pains come and when you're horny for the wrong one. You might want it, but we must want Christ Jesus more. The Lord Jesus Christ was so serious about your body that he prepared a body and wrapped himself in that body to die on the cross to save you – not just from sin. He also came to heal you from every insecurity that has caused you to sabotage every area of your life.

Self-Confidence vs. Christ-Confidence

Self-confidence loves to be fit and in shape and accept the attention and compliments that accompany them. A self-confident individual will not sleep with everyone but might pick the "wrong right." A Christ-confident individual takes care of their body because they are well aware of how much damage was done to Jesus's body for them. A Christ-confident individual will not call themselves ugly because someone called them ugly. They have learned to see themselves the way Christ sees them. A Christ–confident individual realizes that if Jesus died for them when they were not even an embryo yet, they are somebody because God makes no joke.

AFTERWORD

You're the One I Was Looking For

¹⁰ In the same way, all seven of Jesse's sons were presented to Samuel. But Samuel said to Jesse, "The LORD has not chosen any of these." ¹¹ Then Samuel asked, "Are these all the sons you have?" "There is still the youngest," Jesse replied. "But he's out in the fields watching the sheep and goats." "Send for him at once," Samuel said. "We will not sit down to eat until he arrives."

¹² So Jesse sent for him. He was dark and handsome, with beautiful eyes. And the LORD said, "This is the one; anoint him" (1 Samuel 16:10-12, NLT).

David was rejected, overlooked, and not accepted by some of his family. However, God told the prophet, Samuel, that David was the one. He did not look like the one, but he was the one. He did not talk like the one, but he was the one. He did not dress like the one, but he was the one. If for no other reason – GOD SAID HE WAS THE ONE! What made David the one was that he was after God's own heart (1 Samuel 13:14/Acts 13:22). A man after gods heart does not mean that he had Gods heart because only Jesus Christ is God. What made David a man after God's own heart was that he chased after the heart of God. Yes, he felt insecure. Yes, he had a rough childhood, but he chased after God. Yes, he had to grow up quickly, but he chased after God. Yes, he backslid and plotted another man's murder, but he chased after God. Yes, he did not always keep his word, but he chased God. He chased after God until he found out that God is the one!

Yes, Jesus is the one because Jesus is God in the flesh. Jesus is the father in creation, the son of God in redemption, and He is the Holy Spirit in the church and inside the believer. Everything God is dwells in Jesus (Colossians 2:9).

If you want to know this one God, whose name is Jesus:

> *"Then Peter said unto them, Repent, and be baptized every one of you in the name of Jesus Christ for the remission of sins, and ye shall receive the gift of the Holy Ghost"* (Acts 2:38, KJV).

**There's an elephant in the church
that's not being confronted...**

And it's UNHEALED HEARTS!

Elder Curtis Bracy's first book, *Holy Spirit Therapy*, is written to help the reader understand three things:

1. How to deal with wounds that linger, even after being Spirit-filled.
2. How the Holy Spirit is more reliable than power. He's also a comforter.
3. How to trust the Holy Spirit after being betrayed by people in and outside of the church.

"This book is for anyone regardless of how far you are in your spiritual walk. We all need help from the ultimate Help Giver, The Holy Spirit! This read is relatable and understandable. You will put this book down feeling encouraged & ready to face your everyday obstacles. The author challenges us to look to the Holy Spirit for all our needs! Definitely recommend!"
—Ebonee S., Amazon Reviewer

AVAILABLE ON

amazon.com

ABOUT THE AUTHOR

Curtis T. Bracy is a fiery, passionate, spirit-filled preacher who believes the Bible to be true in totality. Bracy is an Ordained Elder in the Church of Our Lord Jesus Christ of the Apostolic Faith, Inc. Bracy serves his pastor and church family at Lighthouse Temple COOLJC. Curtis Bracy holds a B.A. degree in psychology, studied business management, and a master's degree in counseling, concentrating on marriage, family, & couples counseling. Bracy is an apologist for the apostles doctrine. He is a highly sought-after preacher who believes in his God and Savior, the Lord Jesus Christ, the Almighty.